W9-CBS-752

HIKING

MOUNT HOOD

National Forest

Marcia Sinclair

HIKING

MOUNT HOOD

National Forest

Marcia Sinclair

Frank Amato

PORTLAND

Acknowledgments

*For Dean and Simon because they
walk life's trails with me.
Many people gave their gracious
assistance and enthusiastic support
to this project.*

Thanks to Stan Hinatsu for giving my phone number to Frank Amato Publications. Thank you Mary Ellen Fitzgerald, Jim Thornton, Jacqueline Oaks, and Sue Short for sharing your intimate knowledge of the trail system across this forest. Thanks to Jan Prior, Kathleen Martin, Cora Lee Gross and Jeff Jaqua for sharing the rich history of this fascinating place. Thanks to Darcy Morgan, Carol Haugk, Jerry Mills, Ben Smith, Pam Duncan, and Elaine St. Marten who are the grossly underappreciated and endlessly helpful information staff of Mt. Hood National Forest. Thanks Jeff Uebel for teaching me about fish. Thank you Carolyn James of Oregon Department of Transportation for historical information on the old Mt. Hood Loop Highway. Thanks to Bud Schertel from the National Association of Civilian Conservation Corps Alumni for finding that wonderful photo. Thanks Dan Sherman and Carole Hallett of Hawkwatch International, the people who are working hard on behalf of big beautiful raptors. Thanks Doug Anderson for sharing your love of rocks. Dick Robbins

Photo by The gals from The Dalles.

Douglas Asters and the author.

you shared great information about Bull Run Watershed. Thanks Steve Valley for looking out for the dragonflies. Robin Dobson and Barbara Robinson, your photographs of the wildflowers under the oaks are fantastic. I consulted hundreds of research papers and reference books in preparing this book. I am grateful to their authors for providing invaluable information and for vastly widening my view of and appreciation for Mt. Hood National Forest. My sincere thanks to all of you. If I have overlooked mentioning anyone please forgive me.

© 2002 Marcia Sinclair

All rights reserved. No part of this book may reproduced in any means without the written consent of the publisher, except in the case of brief excerpts in critical reviews and articles.

Published in 2002 by
Frank Amato Publications, Inc.
P.O. Box 82112 • Portland, Oregon 97282 • (503) 653-8108
Softbound ISBN: 1-57188-271-5 • Softbound UPC: 0-66066-00460-4
Photography by Marcia Sinclair except where otherwise noted
Book Design: Esther Poleo
Photo Cover: Mount Hood National Forest

Printed in Hong Kong

CONTENTS

MAP *p.6*
ABOUT THIS BOOK *p.8*
INTRODUCTION *p.12*

I MT. HOOD WEST — *p.16*

Salmon River, Sandy River, Bull Run River

1 MCINTYRE RIDGE *p.17*
Bear Grass and Rhodies

2 SALMON RIVER TRAIL *p.19*
Perfect Habitat for Amazing Fish

3 HUNCHBACK MOUNTAIN *p.23*
Roosevelt's Tree Army--The C.C.C.

4 BURNT LAKE TRAIL *p.27*
A Legacy of Fire

5 RAMONA FALLS TRAIL *p.30*
Lahars and Buried Forests

6 PACIFIC CREST TRAIL AT LOLO PASS *p.34*
Peering into the Bull Run

7 LOST LAKE SHORE *p.37*
The Perfect Campsite

8 LITTLE ZIGZAG FALLS *p.40*
A Rest Stop on the Old Highway

9 MIRROR LAKE *p.44*
Popular To A Fault

10 VEDA LAKE *p.47*
Fish In the Clouds

11 TIMBERLINE TRAIL *p.51*
The Trail to Paradise
The Rainshadow
Scoured by Glaciers

II MT. HOOD EAST — *p.58*

White River and Hood River Watersheds

12 GRAVE TRAIL *p.59*
The Barlow Road Section of the Old
Oregon Trail

13 ELK MEADOWS LOOP *p.62*
The Subalpine Parkland

14 HEATHER CANYON *p.65*
The Mountain's Flowered Skirt

15 PARKDALE LAVA BEDS *p.70*
Black Rocks and Red Apples

16 HIGH PRAIRIE *p.74*
A Room With A View

17 SCHOOL CANYON,
LITTLE BADGER CREEK *p.80*
Schooling in Native Plants

18 CRANE PRAIRIE, BOULDER LAKE *p.84*
Wet Meadow Habitat

19 BONNEY BUTTE *p.90*
Soaring Raptors

20 BONNEY MEADOW *p92*
Healing Plants

III CLACKAMAS RIVER NORTH — *p.96*

Oak Grove Fork, Roaring River

21 MEMALOOSE LAKE *p.97*
Forest Succession
and Plant Communities

22 CLACKAMAS RIVER *p102*
A Wild and Scenic River

23 ALDER FLAT *p.106*
An Ancient Grove

24 BLACK WOLF MEADOWS, ANVIL LAKE *p110*
The Seasonal Round

25 MILLER TRAIL, HEADWATERS TRAIL *p114*
Guarding the Forest

26 LITTLE CRATER LAKE *p.117*
Opaline Waters

27 PACIFIC CREST TRAIL *p.122*
The McQuinn Strip

IV CLACKAMAS RIVER SOUTH — *p.126*

Headwaters Collawash, Hot Springs Fork

28 RIVERSIDE TRAIL *p.127*
The Clackamas People's River

29 BAGBY HOT SPRINGS *p130*
A Healing Soak

30 BULL OF THE WOODS *p.133*
The Forces of Nature

31 OLALLIE LAKE *p.138*
Lakes, Views and Huckleberries

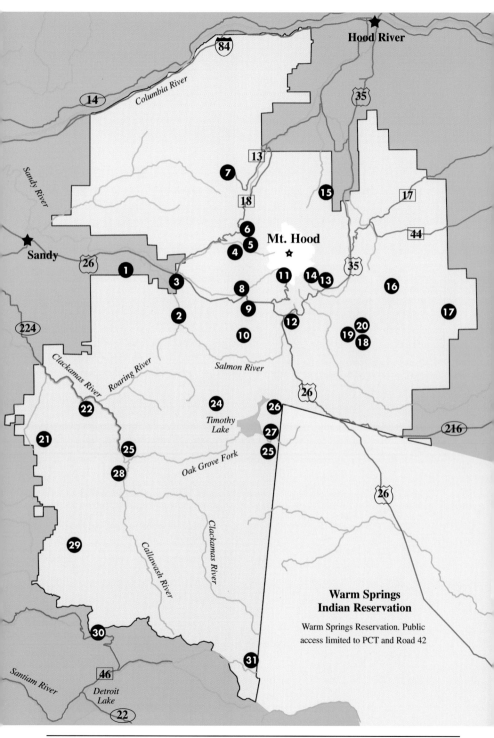

Mt. Jefferson towers over anglers on Olallie Lake.

Trail No.

1 McIntyre Ridge

2 Salmon River Trail

3 Hunchback Mountain

4 Burnt Lake Trail

5 Ramona Falls Trail

6 Pacific Crest Trail at Lolo Pass

7 Lost Lake Shore

8 Little Zigzag Falls

9 Mirror Lake

10 Veda Lake

11 Timberline Trail

12 Grave Trail

13 Elk Meadows Loop

14 Heather Canyon

15 Parkdale Lava Beds

16 High Prairie

17 School Canyon, Little Badger Creek

18 Crane Prairie, Boulder Lake

19 Bonney Butte

20 Bonney Meadow

21 Memaloose Lake

22 Clackamas River

23 Alder Flat

24 Black Wolf Meadows, Anvil Lake

25 Miller Trail, Headwaters Trail

26 Little Crater Lake

27 Pacific Crest Trail

28 Riverside Trail

29 Bagby Hot Springs

30 Bull of the Woods

31 Olallie Lake

About this Book

Hiking Mt. Hood National Forest is a different kind of hiking guide. It is filled with facts, stories and tidbits intended to enlarge your understanding of this place, and in so doing, deepen your experience. I've tried to include what I consider to be the best trails from across the forest in hopes of representing well this vast and varied landscape. Each trail tells a story. In some cases the story is specific to the site, such as raptor migration over Bonney Butte (Hike #19). In some cases, the trail was chosen because it was an ideal place to see, feel or otherwise experience a larger theme, such as Indian seasonal gathering at Black Wolf Meadow (Hike #24). These are the stories of Mt. Hood National Forest, of the waters that flow through it; of the organisms great and small that live in the forest; of the stones and soil that support them; and the adventures and tragedies of the people who have shared this place for thousands of years.

Because this book is primarily an interpretive guide, I have included limited descriptions of the trails themselves. That information is readily available through the Forest Service, from maps, and in traditional hiking guides. Many hiking guide books provide complete descriptions of the trail tread, mileage, elevation gain, and viewpoints. They are helpful for anticipating how much time and energy it will take to find the experience you are seeking. I highly recommend that you consult these other sources before embarking on any of the lengthy or remote hikes in this book.

Always call the nearest Forest Service information center before heading out on a hike. This forest is a dynamic place. Roads wash out, trees fall, and rocks tumble. You may find yourself unable to get to your destination, or on a trail that has not been cleared of debris for several years. This can take the joy out of a hike or worse, jeopardize your safety.

I've given you my assessment of the difficulty of each hike. This is based on my own experience as well as information developed by trails staff of Mt. Hood National Forest. This information is subjective and should be used in combination with other sources of information and a realistic assessment of your abilities. Some of these hikes are in wilderness and other remote areas. Weather can change abruptly. Use common sense and be prepared for changing conditions.

I have recommended the fall season for many hikes, as I think it is an exquisitely beautiful time of the year and the forest is quiet and free from crowds. However, it is hunting season, so please use caution when hiking. Bow hunting season, which starts August 25, doesn't concern me too much. But when deer, bear and cougar seasons begin September 29, an element of madness enters the forest, remaining there through elk season in October and November. Be careful. Wear bright clothes when hiking this time of year and if you hear gunfire, find a safer place.

MAPS

Maps are our friends. They can teach us how the landscape fits together and how it works. They help us make connections we cannot make if we view the forest only from its road system. And a map is indispensable if you take a wrong turn while driving or hiking. If you are not comfortable using one, buy one and practice with it. As you gain familiarity with your map, you will begin to learn how to read it and use it.

I have recommended at least one map for each of the trails. Take a look at the maps offered by the Forest Service, Green Trails, Geo-Graphics and the United States Geological Survey (U.S.G.S). They vary a lot in scale and utility. You will discover for yourself which one is best for you. I have found the Geo-Graphics map particularly helpful, as one side shows the Mt. Hood Wilderness, while the other offers a more expansive view of the entire Mt. Hood Recreation Area. Green Trails produces compact 11x17-inch maps and updates them frequently. I recommend you pack along the Mt. Hood National Forest map for every hike because it is the most up-to-date source of information on the national forest road system. National forest maps are also updated every few years. Mt. Hood National Forest is due for a new one at this writing. If you really love detailed maps, you can pick up a blue line "fireman's" map at ranger stations, the Mt. Hood Information Center and Nature of the Northwest. These show topography and often include the most recent road changes, but the topo lines and roads are drawn to such detail that it appears rather dense. I've also suggested the DeLorme *Oregon Atlas & Gazetteer*. This detailed book of maps for the whole

state is very useful for highway travel and important for exploring areas adjacent to Mt. Hood National Forest that do not appear on the national forest map.

ELEVEN ESSENTIALS

I know you've heard it all before, but it really is important to be prepared when you head out on a hike. The eleven essentials are the items you should always carry with you, even on an easy day hike. I keep most of the necessary items in my day pack so that I don't have to mess around with a lot of preparation when I want to go on a hike. Obviously if you are headed out overnight or longer, careful preparation can mean the difference between a joyous adventure and disaster. Even on a short easy midsummer hike, I do not leave the trailhead without these items:

1. Extra clothing: fleece or wool that can be layered over what I'm wearing. Rain gear.
2. Extra food: enough so that something is left at the end of the trip.
3. Full water bottle(s): all the water I will need for my hike, or a water- purifying device.
4. Knife: great for slicing cheese, but included for first aid and making kindling.
5. Fire starter: candle or lighter to start a fire in damp fuel.
6. Wooden matches with tips dipped in wax in waterproof container.
7. First-aid kit.
8. Topographic map(s).
9. Flashlight with extra batteries and bulb.
10. Compass.
11. Sunscreen: I have survived melanoma, a very aggressive and deadly form of skin cancer. While you won't find sunscreen on other lists of

essentials, I maintain that full-spectrum sunscreen can save your life. Slather it on before you head out, carry a bottle with you and use a sunscreen lip balm, too.

NORTHWEST FOREST PASS

You will need a Northwest Forest Pass trail park permit to park at many of the trailheads listed in this book. The permit is not available at the trailhead, but must be purchased at one of the Forest Service offices listed below or one of a number of private vendors. You can find out who sells them and even order one on-line at the Nature of the Northwest website. The permit card must hang over the interior rear view mirror while you are parked at the trailhead. You can buy a pass for just a day or for the full calendar year. If you do any amount of hiking in Oregon and Washington, the annual pass makes the most sense as it can be used in Pacific Northwest national forests and the North Cascades National Park Complex. You will need it at many national forest campgrounds, boat launches, and visitor centers, too. The fees from the sale of these passes are used to maintain trails and facilities.

Some people grouse about having to pay for the use of national forest trails. In reply, I say that the people who design, build and maintain trails across this rugged landscape have done an incredible job. Most of the trails listed in this book are in great condition. In recent years, trail maintenance budgets have been slashed while the population of Oregon, and Oregonians' love of hiking, continue to grow. On a number of occasions I've encountered trail crews cheerily cutting brush or repairing water bars in 90-degree heat, on near vertical ground, swarmed by mosquitos.

I love these people! Most of these folks are contract crews or volunteers, which helps stretch the trail maintenance budget. Nevertheless, the Forest Service trails staff needs all the help they can get. I applaud their efforts and encourage you to support them with this small investment in the magnificent national forest trail system we take so for granted.

RANGER STATIONS AND INFORMATION OFFICES

The Forest Service has a long history of constantly reorganizing itself. Since 1905, it has changed ranger district names and boundaries on a regular

Ripe Mt. Ash berries.

Mt. Hood framed by rhododendrons.

Photo by Tom Iraci

10 About This Book

Photo by Michael Doke

Apple and pear trees bloom in Hood River Valley.

basis and it continues to do so. This makes it tricky to figure out where to call for information on a specific trail. Don't let this stop you from calling! Helpful information specialists will tell you what you need to know or direct you to someone who can. At this writing, recreation information is available at these locations:

DUFUR RANGER STATION
Barlow Ranger District
P.O. Box 67
Dufur, Oregon 97021
(541) 647-2291

CLACKAMAS RIVER VISITOR CENTER
Estacada Ranger Station
595 N.W. Industrial Way
Estacada, Oregon 97023
(503) 630-8700

HOOD RIVER RANGER STATION
6780 Highway 35
Mt. Hood–Parkdale, Oregon 97041
(541) 352-6002

MT. HOOD INFORMATION CENTER
65000 E. Highway 26
Welches, Oregon 97067
(503) 622-7674 or (503) 622-3360

NATURE OF THE NORTHWEST
800 N.E. Oregon, Suite 177
Portland, Oregon 97232
(503) 872-2750

Lost Lake and Mt. Hood.

Introduction

What if I told you that you own over a million acres of some of the most spectacular real estate in America? On your property, there are cathedral forests of ancient and massive conifer trees. Icy streams, flowing from meadows of dancing wildflowers, tumble together into magnificent rivers. Entire hillsides of wild huckleberries ripen in the August sun.

It is the ancient homeland of a prosperous and gracious people. They witnessed one of the greatest human migrations in all of history when Oregon Trail pioneers passed through their land along the Barlow Road. This land is a major seasonal migration route for thousands of birds of prey, and some of its rare plants are found nowhere else on earth.

There is a majestic snow-covered mountain peak right in the middle of your property, from which you can view all of your domain, including seven other major volcanic peaks and countless smaller mountains in two states. If you weary of surveying your land, you can have a restful soak in your own natural hot springs.

The truth is, you do own this land. It is Mt. Hood National Forest and it belongs to the citizens the United States, to every one of us.

■ THE MOUNTAIN

Oregonians never tire of viewing the big snowy peak the Indians called Wy'east. Its familiar image elicits a joyous response each time it comes into view. To Portlanders, Mt. Hood is the city's elegant backdrop and its favorite playground. Portland's urban planners even restrict building height across the city's skyline to maintain a postcard view of Mt. Hood from established viewpoints in Washington Park.

Portland treasures its mountain view.

Viewed from the north in Hood River, the mountain rises above apple and pear orchards that grow in its rich volcanic soils and are watered by its snow melt. Viewed from the dry open grasslands and wheat fields to the east, Mt. Hood holds the rains and the tourists at bay. It is the mountain that joins northern Oregonians together, and the mountain that defines our distinct communities. The mountain belongs to us all.

■ THE FOREST

It is hard not to dwell in superlatives when describing the forests of Oregon. The massive trees that define this region are legendary in their height and girth. By far the most familiar of these is the mighty Douglas fir. In a class with other Oregon icons like leaping salmon in roaring waterfalls and volcanoes draped in capes of ice, broken-topped Douglas-fir trees rising from a misty mountainside are a classic symbol of Oregon's wild spirit.

The Douglas fir also produces strong beautiful straight-grained structural lumber, making it our most highly prized tree and begetting another Oregon icon, the plaid-shirted logger. Douglas fir rose in value only after settlers brought steel saws and axes. Up to that time, western redcedar was by far the Northwest's most utilitarian tree, used by West Coast Indians for everything from roof shingles to baby diapers.

Unlike most rainforests, in ours the conifers far outnumber the broadleaf deciduous trees and for good reason. Think about a tree and its needs. Deciduous trees send out their food-producing leaves in spring and grow during the warm summer months. They lose their leaves in fall and stay dormant during the cold winter months. But in the Pacific Northwest, much of the life-giving rain falls during that dormant season. Trees have little water when they have sun and little light when they have water.

Evergreen trees with needles are far better suited to our deluge vs. drought climate than their deciduous counterparts. Millions of needles on each tree provide vast surface area for collecting light during the dark winter months, collecting moisture from humid air, and conserving both moisture and nutrients during drought. They grow year round, so they take advantage of the wet season. Douglas firs store huge amounts of water in their big trunks. A mature tree may have bark nearly a foot thick, which helps it retain water and protects it from fire.

Twenty-two other conifers and more than a dozen broadleaf trees define the wide variety of habitats and beautiful woodland scenes across this forest. Each species of tree has preferences in growing conditions, including seasonal temperature highs and lows, rainfall, and soil type. From valley bottom to timberline, the trees sort themselves into zones based on the wide array of conditions found in this varied landscape.

Ecologists have classed these forest zones by the species of trees that continue reproducing in them over time. The trees that continue to sprout and grow in a mature forest are those that are happy growing in shade. In theory, the most shade-tolerant trees would ultimately take over the forest. But forests in Oregon rarely reach this stage called "climax" because fires, wind storms and chain saws halt this process and start the succession of species all over again.

The Riverside Trail is in the Western Hemlock zone.

However, ecologists define the five forested zones in Mt. Hood National Forest by their most shade-tolerant tree. They are Western Hemlock, Grand Fir, Ponderosa Pine, Pacific Silver Fir and Mt. Hemlock.

To look at Mt. Hood National Forest, you would think most of it would fall within the Douglas-fir zone. While Doug firs live a long time and grow to massive proportions, dominating much of the lower-elevation forest, they do have one significant weakness. Doug-fir saplings don't like shade. In a mature forest, as big Douglas firs fall from old age, wind, lightning, or disease, the trees that sprout to replace them are the ones that can grow in shade. Because of this, the centuries-old low-elevation forests eventually are dominated by western hemlock, not Douglas fir. By the ecologist's definition then, the Douglas Fir Zone, where these sun-loving trees do reproduce indefinitely, is found mostly east of the Cascades and along the hot sunny stretches of the Willamette River, but not in Mt. Hood National Forest.

The Western Hemlock Zone covers the relatively warm and moist lower west and south side of Mt. Hood National Forest. Here Douglas fir and western redcedar are western hemlock's most common companions. In this zone, you'll also find noble and grand fir, western yew, big leaf maple, Douglas and vine maple, red alder and Pacific dogwood. A few sugar pines in the upper Clackamas define the northern limits of that tree's range.

Stretching across lowest elevations east of the Cascade crest, the Ponderosa Pine Zone is the warmest and driest in this forest. Summer drought and frequent natural fires maintain this zone of widely spaced trees in a grassy parklike

setting. In such fire-prone land, the ponderosas that reach maturity are the ones that grow at some distance from others, because fires are fueled by closely-spaced young trees and needles dropped from mature trees. The trees that are widely spaced are more likely to reach an age at which thick bark will provide fire protection. Generally, stands in this zone are pure p. pine, although at the lowest elevations Oregon white oak grows in the transition zone between forest and eastern grassland. Lodgepole pine enjoys chilly frost pockets at this elevation.

The pines reach into a higher-elevation band, joining grand fir and Doug fir. This is the Grand Fir Zone, found at moderate elevations east of the Cascade crest. In dry warm conditions, its mix of trees also includes juniper and western larch.

The Pacific Silver Fir Zone occupies the cooler slightly higher western slopes of Mt. Hood, from about 3,000- to 5000-foot elevation and part of the east side of the mountain above 4500 feet. In this varied zone, plant communities range widely from moist protected areas to exposed upper-elevation outcrops. Pacific silver fir may be joined by Douglas, noble, subalpine, grand and white firs; Engelmann spruce; Alaskan yellow cedar; western redcedar; western larch; white bark, lodgepole and western white pines; and western and mountain hemlock. It is a land of heavy snows, where stands of Sitka alder define the paths of avalanches.

In the band of highest-elevation forested parklands, in a region that gets the heaviest snow loads in the world, the slender gnarled profile of mountain hemlock gives little purchase to the snows that dominate its life. Defining this zone, mountain hemlock grows in cold temperatures and coarse soils, spending more than half the year under a heavy snow pack. Within its zone, whitebark pine and subalpine larch withstand the austere conditions. Alaska yellow cedar grows in moist north-facing sites and exposed ridges in this zone, demarcating avalanche chutes. Above it on the high ridges, small clusters of sub-alpine firs scratch out a living in gritty natural rock gardens and dry meadows that form the timberline of Mt. Hood.

A LAND DEFINED BY WATER

Mt. Hood National Forest is a landscape of fantastic contrasts. Rain falls in buckets here for nine months, then abruptly stops from July to September. On the west side of the mountain, rain-drenched forests drink up over one hundred inches of annual precipitation. Giant cedars soak their feet in moss-covered bogs. River-bottom old growth maintains its hushed dewy shade year round. On the east side of the Cascade Range, in the mountain's rain shadow, crackling pine and oak forests make miserly use of their meager twenty inches of annual rain. Gnarled and stunted junipers cling to parched rocks and tiny gray-green succulents keep leaves small and stems low to conserve every molecule of moisture.

This landscape rises from near sea level at the Columbia River Gorge to the 11,245-foot summit of Mt. Hood. The big peak is a stratovolcano, a pile of volcanic

ash and boulders loosely held together by lava and ice. Its deep winter snows and ancient ice fields melt slowly in the springtime sunlight, and flow down its face, carving steep valleys. Creeks that run cold and clear tumble through the forest to feed major regional rivers that define its boundaries—the Columbia on the north, the Willamette on the west, the North Santiam on the south and the Deschutes on the east.

Water shapes the contours of this landscape. To help you explore this magnificent forest, I have divided it into four regions, each of which contains several watersheds. The roads that carry you to your destination for the most part follow the course of rivers that, over eons, defined the landscape and its character. You will gain an entirely different relationship to this place when you begin to think of it not from its constructed travel corridors, but by the way that water and other natural elements flow through it.

Snow fields thaw in late-spring sun.

MOUNT HOOD WEST
Salmon River, Sandy River, Bull Run River

1 McIntyre Ridge Trail#782 *p.17*
Bear grass and rhodies

2 Salmon River Trail *p.19*
Perfect habitat for amazing fish

3 Hunchback Mountain *p.23*
Roosevelt's tree army--The C.C.C.

4 Burnt Lake Trail *p.27*
A legacy of fire

5 Ramona Falls Trail *p.30*
Lahars and buried forests

6 Pacific Crest Trail
at Lolo Pass *p.34*
Peering into the Bull Run

7 Lost Lake *p.37*
The perfect campsite

8 Little Zigzag Falls Trail *p.40*
A rest stop on the old highway

9 Mirror Lake *p.44*
Popular to a fault

10 Veda Lake *p.47*
Fish in the clouds

11 Timberline Trail *p.51*
The Trail to Paradise The Rainshadow scoured by glaciers

McIntyre Ridge

Trail #782
Bear Grass and Rhodies

Recommended Seasons: Summer, Fall
Use: Light
Difficulty: Moderate

■ MAPS

Mount Hood National Forest, Geo-Graphics Mt. Hood Wilderness, Bull of the Woods and Salmon Huckleberry Wilderness, Green Trails Cherryville #460.

■ DIRECTIONS

Take U.S. Highway 26 ten miles east of Sandy. Watch for a service station on the south side of the road. At this writing, it is a 76 station. Just past the station, turn right onto Wildcat Creek Road. At 1 1/2 miles go left, in another 7/10 mile go left again, then in 1 1/3 miles go right. The trailhead is in another 3/4 of a mile.

McIntyre Ridge is one of several high-ridgeline trails in the Zigzag area. The trail begins in a Bureau of Land Management clearcut, but soon crosses the national forest boundary into Douglas-fir forest. The trail skirts the northwestern border of the Salmon Huckleberry Wilderness. At the junction to Wildcat Butte, the trail enters the wilderness. The ridge and trail were named for the McIntyre family who ran the Brightwood store. A section of the old Mt. Hood Loop Highway just east of Brightwood was called McIntyre Hill.

This trail offers several glimpses of Mt. Hood in the first few miles, but 2 1/2 miles into the hike, the forest opens and you are treated to an exquisite view of the mountain in all its glory. While there are plenty of nice hikes around with views of Mt. Hood, schedule this one from middle June to the first part of July because that's when the rhododendrons are in bloom.

Pacific rhododendron, the state flower of Washington, is a hardy evergreen shrub that grows in montane forests from British Columbia to California. In the shade of the woods, it grows tall enough to qualify as a small tree, developing a leggy architecture and shiny zucchini-green leaves. In the open, it remains compact and dense with gray-green leaves.

Related to azalea, heather, salal and huckleberry, it prefers sites with shallow soil, summer drought and low nutrients. For this reason, it is common in areas that have been burned by hot forest fires. The ridges on either side of Highway 26 were burned repeatedly in the early 1900s, becoming prime sites for rhododendron. In fact, some south-facing slopes on these mountains, where hot air shimmers in August, refuse to sprout anything but rhodies. Once established, dense thickets allow few other shrubs or trees to take up residence.

Although it may be a bit territorial, we forgive all when *Rhododendron macrophylum* puts on its show in early summer. Here on McIntyre Ridge, that show is unsurpassed. Each bush may have several clusters of blossoms. Surrounded by whorls of large leathery leaves, clusters of five-petaled flowers with ruffled edges range from true pink to deep rose. One upper petal on each flower is dusted with brown speckles and the throat is splash with yellow.

Beautifully synchronized, bear grass joins the show, opening thousands of tiny white blooms on swaying wands up to four feet tall. The tuft of leaves at the base provides a valuable material for Indian baskets and is used in commercial flower arrangements. Not a grass at all, bear grass is in the lily family. It, too, grows in places where the soil is low in nutrients and blooms prolifically after a fire. After several fire-free seasons, it blooms every two to three years. Peer at a single flower cluster to see the tiny bees and hover flies getting giddy on bear grass nectar.

McIntyre Ridge trail is the shortest way into the north side of the Salmon Huck Wilderness. It connects with several other ridgeline trails so you can create a variety of longer loops, particularly if you set up a car or bike shuttle. There is no water on the trail, so fill up those water bottles in advance. Also, there are a few places where the trail is difficult to follow, particularly after that first big Mt. Hood View. Don't get so dazzled by the view that you lose your way.

■ OTHER HIKING OPTIONS

Plaza Trail #783 goes up Huckleberry Mountain

from Wildwood Recreation site.

Douglas Trail #781 joins Plaza and McIntyre trail via Wildcat Mountain.

Bear grass wands wave in the June breeze.

Glimpse of Mt. Hood from McIntyre Ridge trail.

Salmon River

National Recreation Trail #742
Perfect Habitat for Amazing Fish

Recommended Seasons: Spring, Summer, Fall
Use: Extra heavy first five miles, then medium
Difficulty: Easy

MAPS

Mount Hood National Forest, Bull of the Woods Wilderness and Salmon Huckleberry Wilderness.

DIRECTIONS

From U.S. Highway 26 near Welches, turn south on Salmon River Road, Forest Road 2618, and follow it five miles to the trailhead. The Old Salmon River Trail runs between the river and road for 2 1/2 miles.

Driving east on Highway 26 past Brightwood, the topography becomes very striking. You are driving past the confluence of several major rivers and creeks that have sculpted a steep and rugged terrain. The Sandy River enters from the north at Lolo Pass Road, rushing along the foot of Zigzag Mountain. The Salmon River flows toward it from the south, tumbling between Salmon and Hunchback mountains. Still Creek and the Zigzag River rush toward you from the east, running roughly parallel to the highway.

For years, I was so focused on the highway, I barely noticed the terrain. Make a point of noticing. These steep forested slopes, flat gravel river beds, and their icy waters combine to provide excellent habitat for our most splendid and endangered wild salmon.

Turn south at Salmon River Road and drive up the river canyon to the Salmon River Trailhead. Your hike begins in a humid, mossy old-growth forest of Douglas-fir and western redcedar. Designated as a National Recreation Trail, it follows the Salmon River upstream through a deep river canyon in

Ancient cedar stumps grow a moss garden.

the Salmon Huckleberry Wilderness.

In the first few miles, you're likely to see hikers with fishing gear and little tufted hooks in their hats and vests. If you happen on a skilled fly-fisher hip deep in the river, pause and watch the show. A beautifully executed cast is like an elegant dance step, as shifting arm and shoulder muscles send the glistening, gossamer line floating through shafts of sparkling sunlight.

Of the nine salmon-like species that inhabit the Pacific Northwest, four traditionally lived in the Salmon River. Chinook, steelhead, coho and cutthroat trout are "anadromous," meaning they hatch in fresh water, migrate to the ocean, then return to fresh water to reproduce. Today, our wild anadromous fish are in trouble. Their populations over recent years have plummeted. Some of the causes for this decline are

evident here on the Salmon River. To grasp their decline it helps to understand these fish.

Starting as glacier thaw high on Mt. Hood, the Salmon River gathers momentum as it tumbles through mountain rain forest, then joins the Sandy River and glides through agricultural valley lands before pouring into the Columbia. The conditions for fish are extremely varied from headwaters to mouth. Each species and even each subspecies or "stock" has evolved an effective survival strategy by using a specific part of the stream at a specific time of the year.

Fall chinook need deep pools and live in the lower main stem. There are still fall chinook in the lower Sandy River and some in the Salmon River. Spring chinook arrive in spring, find large deep holes, park, and wait out the summer. Most of these hiding spots are

Photo by Brian O'Keefe.

Rainbow trout.

in the lower main stem and tributaries. As the first autumn raindrops cool the parched land, they emerge and spawn. Juveniles spend a year in fresh water before striking out for the ocean.

Coho prefer the easy pace of smaller streams, or placid main stem side channels. They are not well suited to the upper part of the river. Coho have suffered the greatest habitat loss, because most habitat is now on private land in the lower Sandy. There may not be enough coho left to list them as endangered.

Steelhead like riffles and step pools of moderate and small streams.

Cutthroat prefer the smallest, highest tributaries. Here in the Salmon, cutthroat migrated higher and higher upstream. Debris from volcanoes and abrasive glacier-rock dust cut the stream channel deeper, creating higher falls. Now Salmon River cutthroat are landlocked, trapped above geologic barriers.

Salmon are among the most adaptable creatures on earth. From fresh water, to salt water they change their entire body chemistry and face a completely foreign environment. Then they change back again, and return to fresh water using a baffling and amazing olfactory navigation to literally "smell their way home" to their natal waters. Against all odds, they have lived in this river for tens of millions of years, adapting to a dynamic environment.

At their birth, these volcanic mountains sent hot ash, pumice, and mud flows down these canyons. When things weren't hot, they were bitter cold. An ice age or two have sent glaciers advancing and receding across the landscape.

While conditions became more stable some 9,000 years ago, the old-growth rain forests of the West are ever changing, renewed by disturbances like fire and wind. Salmon River fish evolved with 300-foot trees crashing into their homes and damming their streams. So well adapted to change, they may still survive the huge and swift changes brought about by humans in the last 150 years.

The Indians of Mt. Hood area gathered food in lands of the Salmon Huckleberry Wilderness. They collected enough food for a season's use, and traded away any surplus. But Euro-American settlers viewed the vast number of migrating salmon as unlimited and marketable for profit. Using fish wheels, seines, and nets, they captured so many fish that as early as the 1890s, there were concerns that fish populations were in peril.

In addition, lands that provide the best fish habitat were also best for farmers. Homesteaders secured rich bottom lands, then burned to clear land. Often they lost control of their fires. The west flanks of Mt. Hood were igniting every 20-30 years, where the normal fire cycle is 300 years or more. Exposed soil washed into the rivers, clogging salmon spawning gravel. Settlers logged the banks of Still Creek, Camp Creek, and the Salmon River.

In 1910, the Sandy River was dammed for hydroelectric power. Marmot Dam was only 20 feet high, but at autumn low water levels, fall chinook couldn't pass it. What's more, water was diverted from the Little Sandy to Bull Run River to Roslyn Lake. Juvenile salmon swimming downstream landed in Roslyn Lake and met the dam turbines. Returning adult fish were attracted by odor and sent off course to the Bull Run River.

By then, people were flocking to the forest with fishing poles and pressuring fish-and-game managers to keep streams well stocked. That year 10,000 chinook, steelhead, and coho were released in the Salmon River at Boulder Creek. Fish began spawning earlier because the hatchery fish were bred spawn early to create fishing opportunities year round.

By the 1940s, fire-fighting techniques improved, and the upper Sandy River watershed began to recover. But conditions were deteriorating downstream. Runoff from farms carried sediment, fertilizers, and pesticides. Trees were cleared and water temperatures rose. Then a ten-year drought reduced fish to critically low levels.

So, isn't there any good news in this story? There is. The best hedge against extinction of these fish was the change in the 1990s in forest management that reduced logging and placed greater value on ecosystems. These changes are allowing streams to recover. Stepped-up research has taught us a lot more about salmon. And the listing of fish species under the Endangered Species Act helped secure their future and raised public concern.

Our native anadromous fish have adapted to an astonishing level of change in their habitat. While a few Oregon stocks are considered extinct, there is still hope for most of our native salmon. It is up to us to save them. There are terrific sources of information available to citizens, telling us what we can each do to improve their chances for survival. At a minimum, those of us in western Oregon can take action in our local watersheds to keep toxins and sediment out of our storm drains, and therefore our creeks and rivers. These fish have the tenacity and endurance to survive monumental changes to their world. The least we can do is modify our own to save them.

■ OTHER HIKING OPTIONS

Make your first stop Cascade Streamwatch in the Wildwood Recreation Area in Welches. You start this interpretive trail as a fish, in a clever entry that looks like a streambed, illustrating the important components of stream structure that provide quality habitat. The site includes an underwater viewing structure, wetland, and seasonalopportunities to watch spawning salmon and steelhead. Call (503)375-5646 for information.

Fawn lilies bloom in March and April.

3

Hunchback Mountain

Trail #793

Roosevelt's Tree Army—the C.C.C.

Season: Spring, Summer, Fall
Use: Moderate
Difficulty: Strenuous

MAPS

Mount Hood National Forest, Geo-Graphics Mt. Hood Wilderness, Bull of the Woods Wilderness and Salmon Huckleberry Wilderness.

DIRECTIONS

Take Highway 26 twenty miles west of Sandy to the community of Zigzag. Turn right into the ranger station parking lot, stay left and drive through the parking lot until you see the trailhead sign on the right.

When the stock market crashed in1929, it shocked the nation and left millions of Americans destitute. Bank closures wiped out people's life savings. Millions of workers were left jobless and hopeless. Children were pulled out of school to help their families scrape together a living. By 1933, the nation was desperate. When Franklin Delano Roosevelt took office, in January of that year, he proposed immediate changes to help struggling families. One of the first pieces of legislation he proposed to Congress was the Emergency Conservation Work Act, the law that created the "Civilian Conservation Corps."

The concept was simple. Our national lands needed attention and there were thousands of unemployed young men who needed work. Roosevelt put the two together in the most popular depression-era program—a program that left a legacy of beautifully crafted stonework, wooden structures and forest thoroughfares—a legacy that we treasure today.

Building displays classic C.C.C. style.

This roughskin newt enjoys the cool moist habitat of Hunchback Mountain.

Here's a chance to explore a bit of depression-era history before heading up Hunchback Mountain, the high forested ridge between Still Creek and the Salmon River. The Hunchback Mountain trailhead is located in the parking lot of the ranger station near some of Mt. Hood's best-preserved C.C.C.-era buildings. Breathe the mountain air and imagine what it was like for a young man arriving on his first day of camp.

The C.C.C. recruited young men, age 18 to 25 who were single, unemployed and from families receiving federal assistance. Many of these men lived in East Coast cities and had never been in a forest before. Many were hungry. Providing three square meals a day, skill training, wages, and schooling, Camp Zigzag helped boys with few options and little formal education develop into disciplined, confident and hopeful young men. (At the time Eleanor Roosevelt thought there should be camps for young women as well, but her idea was not pursued.) Each young man received

$30 a month, of which $25 was sent home to his family.

Camp Zigzag #928 was the first C.C.C. camp in Oregon and the last to disband. A few hundred yards up Lolo Pass Road, there is a stone marker with a bronze plaque, placed by Camp 928 alumni in 1998 to mark the site of the work camp that changed their lives between 1933 and 1942. Interestingly, Camp Zigzag was uniquely prepared for their arrival.

The Zigzag Ranger Station was established in 1907 in what was then the Bull Run District. Chosen because the nearby meadow provided pasturage for pack trains, it served as an important Forest Service depot for supplies headed for remote outposts. Most communication between the Portland headquarters and other stations across the forest came through Zigzag.

Oregonians had already discovered this mountain playground before the turn of the century and by the 1920s, work of the ranger station was focused primarily on improving public access to recreation. Zigzag was one of the first ranger stations in the nation to employ a recreation planner, hiring landscape architect Francis Williamson. A prolific designer, he developed plans for the entire highway corridor, including summer home sites, campgrounds, and a 1929 plan for the Zigzag Ranger Station compound. Little did he know that with these plans in place the ranger district was perfectly poised for welcoming the willing workers of the C.C.C.

The ranger station itself was small and rustic when the young C.C.C. recruits arrived. By 1942, men of the C.C.C. had constructed 21 buildings according to Williamson's plan in a traditional military "quad" facing into a center yard. The historic buildings that remain today are all from that C.C.C. period. The road to the Hunchback Mountain trailhead is a small remnant of the old Mt. Hood Loop Highway. The design of the compound was intended to be both functional and welcoming to highway travelers. The diagonal placement of the current ranger station, circa 1966, regrettably ignored the traditional road and building arrangement.

Because of its public visibility, Zigzag was selected as a test site for the "refined rustic" style of architecture developed by Tim Turner, the same architect who designed Timberline Lodge. Unlike the earlier "rustic" style of log cabins and stonework, these buildings were characterized by clapboard, shiplap, and board-and-batten exterior walls, sturdy squared timber archways, shake roofs and the most identifiable feature—shutters with pine-tree cut outs. After trial here, it became the hallmark of Forest Service buildings and the C.C.C. throughout the Pacific Northwest.

The C.C.C. was called "Roosevelt's Tree Army" because of their accomplishments in reforesting burned and logged public lands. In addition to construction of the ranger station, the men of Camp 928 worked on road and trail construction, too. While Works Progress Administration (another Depression-era program) workers built Timberline Lodge, C.C.C. workers constructed the Timberline Loop Road. The rustic stone shelters along the Timberline Trail were built by the C.C.C., as were benches, ditches, and signs for roads and trails. You can still find a few of the old-style hand-carved signs with raised lettering along the Highway 26 corridor. These signs are credited to Larry Espinoza, a C.C.C. woodwork craftsman.

They constructed miles of trails, including the Pioneer Bridle Trail that integrated several sections of Barlow Road. It is located just a few miles east on U.S. 26. (see below) They also built some of our simplest, most elegant, and lasting campgrounds.

If C.C.C. to you means Crazy Cardiovascular Conditioning you'll love Hunchback Mountain. This is not a trail for the faint of heart, or for those who value their knees. The first few yards of this trail are a gentle mosey through moist Douglas-fir forest, then you hit long switchbacks for a mile or so, and then the thigh-burner section—a mile or so straight up. The lower forest is lovely just after a soft rain, but you'll want clear weather when you hit the top for views into the Salmon River watershed to the west and glimpses of Mt. Hood to the east. The trail then connects to a number of trails along a ridge crest roller coaster route. A round trip to Devil's Peak is over 16 miles and very strenuous, but there are several shorter loops if you car or bike shuttle.

■ OTHER HIKING OPTIONS

If you're looking for something a bit more horizontal and want to search out more C.C.C. history, consider hopping on a section of the Pioneer Bridle Trail. The entire route is 8.6 miles and works best as a car shuttle. When the C.C.C built this trail in the 1930s they couldn't have imagined today's high-speed traffic on U.S. 26, which will dominate your experience. Nevertheless, the trail takes you to or near some choice historic spots.

It starts at Forest Road 2620, and runs through Tollgate Campground. There you can admire the group picnic shelter built by the C.C.C. in the early 1930s of peeled log construction with a flagstone floor and large square fireplace. Heading east, the trail continues past the replica of the old Barlow Road Tollgate. It crosses the highway at Forest Road 2639 and continues on the north side. There's an open mine shaft at 6.5 miles, so keep track of the kids. A bit past the mine, you can take a side spur to the Laurel Hill chute—the most infamous section of Barlow Road—or follow abandoned sections of the old Mt. Hood Loop Highway to Little Zigzag Falls Trail (Hike #8). If you follow it for its entire length you'll end between mile posts 52 and 53 across from Mt. Hood Ski Bowl.

Photo from Archives of National Association of Civilian Conservation Corps Alumni.

Webb Harrington and Delmar Westlund on 1937 Camp Zigzag sign.

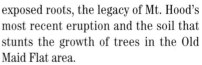

Burnt Lake

Trail #772

A Legacy of Fire

Recommended Season: Summer, Fall
Use: Heavy
Difficulty: Strenuous

■ MAPS

Mount Hood National Forest, Geo-Graphics Mt. Hood Wilderness.

■ DIRECTIONS

From U.S. Highway 26 in Zigzag, turn left (north) on Lolo Pass Road #18. Drive four miles, bear right onto Forest Road 1825, cross the bridge and continue 1.7 miles to a junction. Bear right on 1825 and follow it 3/10 of a mile until the pavement ends. Keep left and bear right on 1825-109. Follow this to the end.

The Burnt Lake Trail begins as a delightful mosey through a lush forest full of bird song and the smell of moist humus. Moss covers the spongy old cedar logs that slowly decompose into the forest duff. Thickets of thimbleberry, salmonberry, oxalis, and bunchberry hint that this is a moist site. But it's the devil's club, that beautiful bramble with the evil thorns, each perfectly angled to gouge skin, that says this area stays wet year round.

Exposed root wads of huge upturned western redcedars show that each of these giants had a shallow root system. Trees here don't have to send their roots far for ample moisture. A gummy, gray, gritty soil covers their exposed roots, the legacy of Mt. Hood's most recent eruption and the soil that stunts the growth of trees in the Old Maid Flat area.

Even on a 95-degree day, the humid shade feels cool. Late in the summer, you'll still find yourself gingerly avoiding mud puddles in the first couple of miles that run between a small stream and Lost Creek. How could a trail this wet lead to a place called Burnt Lake? Look a little closer and you begin to find clues. There aren't many old trees here. As the trail gains elevation, you leave the creek bottom and climb the rocky canyon wall, circling above a graveyard of burned cedar snags. Solemn and stately, some eight feet in diameter, these giants were sculpted into eery works are art, colored in charcoal and weathered to a soft gray.

Climbing the trail into dryer more open forest of rhododendrons and bear grass, a warm breeze carries the smell of wood smoke. Campfires are prohibited at the lake. Could this smoke be from a forest fire?

■ THE FIRE

Ralph Lewis and John Cooper worked for the Forest Service in 1906. Twenty-three years old, they had grown up as children of the first homesteaders living around the mountain. Cooper Spur was named for John Cooper's father who helped build the road up

Above Burnt Lake, hikers enjoy views and huckleberries.

There were no phones and people were spread out across miles of forest. As was the custom then, "winos" were rounded up on Burnside Street in Portland and brought by wagon to the mountain to fight fire.

While rangers tried to round up firefighters, the Clear Creek Fire spread from what is now McNeil Campground east across Old Maid Flat, up Zigzag Mountain and toward Lost Lake. Then the wind shifted. Blowing from the east, it took the fire back across its own path. According to Ralph and John it stopped at "green timber."

This wasn't the first fire through here. A series of fires had swept across the south and west flanks of Mt. Hood starting in 1902. It was in a 1904 blaze that Burnt Lake got its name. Even before these fires came through, the country was open enough that people traveled on foot or horseback through an open understory. The trail from Lost Lake to the Sandy River wasn't built until 1903.

the mountain. Ralph and John named many landmarks in the country between Bull Run Lake and Zigzag Mountain. They knew every stream and rock outcrop. Their colorful story of the Clear Creek Fire was recorded when both men were elderly and is on file at Zigzag Ranger Station.

According to Ralph and John, in late August of 1906 a homesteader near Clear Creek was burning logs. He went out for a Sunday and left the fire burning. A west wind came up and "throwed it" across his fire lines into brush and dead timber. The fire became explosive. The ranger at Clear Fork "lost his head and put all his supplies in the creek and went for help."

Gathering firefighters in 1906 was no small task. There were no roads through this country, only a few trails.

Indians used fire to maintain the plants they used most for food and medicine and sacred ceremonies. They regularly burned the forest late in the season, timing it so that the first fall rains would extinguish the blaze. This cleared shrubs and seedlings, but didn't burn hot enough to kill the larger trees. According to Ralph, "It was said the Indians liked to see things burned off on account of hunting, and people to this day think that if the Indians was running things instead of the Forest Service, we'd have less of these big fires."

By the turn of the century, more people were using the forest for homesteading and recreation. As a result, fires became common during the hot summer months. A 1903 government report on forest conditions in the Cascade Range stated, "These burns have taken place in all parts of the reserve, and are so cannot be attributed to any particular cause, but rather demonstrate that wherever men go fires follow."

By 1906, firefighting had become a Service. That year the rangers at Mt. Hood started posting lookouts. Ralph was one of the first. Thus began a hundred-year history of preventing and controlling forest fires.

AFTER THE FIRE

Forest fires are often described using terms like "catastrophic" and "devastation." But fires are integral to the complex ecology of western forests. Northwest forest ecosystems depend upon forest fires for renewal.

Most fires don't destroy the forest. Cooler fires often follow ridgelines and avoid the damp confines of "riparian" streamside areas, leaving them intact. In moist sites like the lower Burnt Lake Trail, seeds and plants are kept moist and protected, ready to help regenerate the forest. Burned snags provide habitat for birds and insects. Ash provides nutrients for new growth. Some plant species are so well adapted to fire they require a fire's heat to germinate seeds.

Since those early days, land managers have realized that preventing fire doesn't help the forest. Today many national forests in the West are prone to large hot fires because there haven't been the small cooler fires to clear away shrubs and small trees. Fueled by accumulated brush, logs, and duff, a wildfire may burn so hot that nothing grows back for years. To avoid this and to work in harmony with natural processes, controlled or "prescribed" burns are becoming a standard component of forest management and restoration.

BACK ON THE TRAIL...

The Burnt Lake Trail arrives at its picturesque namesake, then mounts a steep hillside leading to a trail junction triangle. From there, Zigzag Mountain Trail offers great views back across the lake to Mt. Hood and promises late-summer huckleberries. Cast Lake is a quieter but equally appealing retreat. Use the Mount Hood Wilderness map for options and check with the Mount Hood Visitor Center for trail conditions.

Crowds vanish midweek at Burnt Lake.

5

Ramona Falls

Trail #797

Lahars and Buried Forests

Recommended Season: Spring, Summer, Fall
Use: Heavy
Difficulty: Moderate

MAPS

Mount Hood National Forest, Geo-Graphics Mt. Hood Wilderness.

DIRECTIONS

From U.S. Highway 26 in Zigzag, drive north on Lolo Pass Road for 4.2 miles, turn right on Road 1825 and in .7 miles turn right across the Sandy River Bridge. In 1.8 miles follow the left fork on Road 100. The parking lot is one half mile ahead.

Ramona Falls skips and tumbles down its black basalt staircase, tossing rainbow mist and glistening droplets in all directions. Like gossamer white fabric, the effervescent water drapes across the dark stone. This is one of the loveliest sites in Mt. Hood National Forest and for that reason, you will rarely find yourself alone at Ramona Falls. Although it is located within Mt. Hood Wilderness, this is not the place to find wilderness solitude. But on summer weekdays and off-season weekends, the crowds disappear. That's the time to head for the falls and enjoy a hike that displays in graphic relief the eruptive power of a young and volatile volcano.

Mt. Hood looks peaceful beneath its snowy blanket, but it has a lively recent history. Within the past 10,000 years, it erupted three times. Geologists named these three eruptive periods Timberline, Zigzag and Old Maid. The Timberline Eruptive Period, over 1400 years ago, sent so much volcanic material down the southwest face of the mountain that it buried its ice-carved topography under a smooth fan of sand and gravel. This fan extends from Crater Rock to the base of the mountain, or what is now Timberline Ski Area and Government Camp. Loose ash mixed with melted snow, formed hot abrasive lahars that filled the Sandy and Zigzag river valleys and created a delta at the mouth of the Sandy River where it joins the Columbia.

The Zigzag Eruptive Period, some 400 to 600 years ago, formed smaller fan-shaped deposits in the upper Sandy River near Ramona Falls.

The Old Maid Eruptive Period began in the 1700s and ended about the time that Lewis and Clark canoed through the Columbia Gorge. In fact, the river we call the Sandy got its name from them. Clark's journal entry from November 3, 1805 describes "Quicksand River," a stream that appeared to be flowing over a wide sandbar and was only four inches deep. "I attempted to wade this Stream and to my astonishment

Finely ground rock makes Sandy River water "milky."

found the bottom a quick sand and impassable." Settlers later shortened the name to Sandy.

To get to the Ramona Falls trailhead, you will drive through Old Maid Flat. It is easy to recognize that you're in an area of volcanic deposits. Old Maid Flat soils are young and not fully developed. The sandy, drought-prone soil is covered with thick moss and lichens. Its forest of stunted pines and fir, with scattered rhododendrons and huckleberry, is in sharp contrast to the moist forests of Douglas fir and cedar on the outskirts of the flats. Old Maid Flat is famous for its wild mushrooms (pickers must get a Forest Service permit), and supports a number of rare plant communities.

Lahars from the Old Maid Period engulfed and entombed old-growth forests on the west side of the mountain. Over the years, winter rains, road construction and river channel changes have exposed snags and stumps, long covered and preserved under ash and sand. Geologists have found six of these prehistoric buried forests near Mt. Hood. Today you can see remains of several of them if you know where to look. The largest of these preserved forests is on this trail.

Ramona Falls Trail starts out as one trail, then splits into a loop. The first section follows the course of the Sandy River. The eroded volcanic ash and grit, crunching with each boot step, makes for slow-going through some sections, like hiking on a dry beach. The river's

From Ramona Creek you'll see the steep south cliffs of Yocum Ridge.

midsummer icy water is milky with suspended glacial "flour," a rock dust ground from the mountain by the weight of Reid Glacier high on Mt. Hood. The Sandy has one of the highest percentages of glacial melt of all the major Oregon rivers.

A bridge at 1.25 miles is helicoptered in each spring and removed each fall, as it can't withstand the early spring torrent of melting snows off the mountain. The trail split comes just shy of 1.5 miles. Continue along the Sandy River to a junction with the Timberline Trail and P.C.T., arriving at the falls at three miles. Ramona Creek supplies the falls with snow melt from Yocum Ridge.

The first half of the return loop offers an entirely different experience, following Ramona Creek's mossy, moist forested banks. It then swings north away from the creek and toward the Muddy Fork of the Sandy River, the well-named flow off the Sandy Glacier. The

Muddy Fork was dammed by glacial debris during the Old Maid Eruptive Period. As you near it, start looking for the buried forest. Thirty to fifty trees are on both sides of the trail near the junction with the Portage Trail #784.

You can tell these trees from present-day snags because they have no swelling at the base where the trunk meets the roots. Often the base is rotted. Run your hand along the trunk and follow it below ground. The trunk will keep going on these buried trees, where a normal tree will send out multiple roots at the ground level.

The well-signed trail guides you back to the trailhead.

■ OTHER OPTIONS

To see more prehistoric buried forests:
From the Paradise Park Trailhead on Forest Road 2639, hike 100 yards up the trail then head cross-country back to the Zigzag River. Trees are exposed in a 25-foot bank along the river. Remains of the old Mt Hood Loop Highway can be seen on the opposite shore.

In Lost Creek Barrier Free Campground, three miles north of Lolo Pass in the Old Maid Flat Area, follow the trail upstream from the parking area for views of well-exposed preserved trees. There are at least 20 and most still have bark. The swampy beaver pond may be a remnant of the small lake formed by a volcanic-debris dam.

Rainbows and mist dance over Ramona Falls.

Pacific Crest Trail at Lolo Pass

Trail #2000

Peering into the Bull Run

Recommended Season: Spring, Summer, Fall
Use: Varies with season
Difficulty: Moderate

■ MAPS

Mount Hood National Forest, Geo-Graphics Mt. Hood Wilderness

■ DIRECTIONS

From U.S. Highway 26, turn north on Lolo Pass Road, Forest Road 18. Drive to the pass and watch for trailhead and P.C.T. signs. Or from Hood River take Highway 35 south, turn west at Dee and follow signs toward Lost Lake. Watch for the junction with Lolo Pass Road.

This section of the Pacific Crest Trail connects the feet of Mt. Hood with the Columbia River Gorge. The trail meanders along the ridge between the Bull Run Watershed and the West Fork of Hood River. At four miles you can take a one-mile spur trail to Lost Lake or continue on to Wahtum Lake or even Cascade Locks.

The first 1/4 mile of this trail is an uphill gravely scramble. But then the trail mellows to a rolling tread through a middle-aged fir forest. Thimbleberry, vine and Douglas maples, and huckleberry offer a verdant array of green hues in spring and summer. Wild flowers add pizazz to the scene.

Come September, pack a thermos of soup, some gingerbread and a fresh apple. This is a gorgeous hike on a breezy fall day, when these same plants have warmed their pallet from greens to golds. Vine maple leaves, backlit by low autumn sun, light up the forest shade. In scree fields, the mid-afternoon rays ignite the huckleberry and maples to a radiant red against charcoal-gray basalt.

Interestingly, within the first half mile from the pass, another shade of yellow appears in the forest—the yellow of metal warning signs with black letters. They say, "No Trespassing. Bull Run Watershed." So here's a sneaky little secret: although you thought that no one is allowed to go into the Bull Run Watershed, Portland's treasured source of drinking water, by golly you're standing in it!

Okay, technically, you're not in the watershed. The Pacific Crest Trail runs through part of the Bull Run Watershed Management Unit, but it lies outside the watershed. And that technicality matters a lot.

A watershed is an area of land in which all the water that enters it drains to one place. Think of it as a bathtub. In the case of the Bull Run Watershed, all the rain and snow and mist that enters the watershed drains to Bull Run River. To protect that water, there is a buffer area surrounding the watershed that is also part of the Management Unit. The P.C.T. is in the buffer, or on the outside rim of the bathtub. To use another plumbing fixture analogy, rain that falls on the trail where you stand drains toward Lost Lake, not toward Portland's kitchen sinks. On the other side of those yellow signs, you're getting into kitchen sink territory.

While the Management Unit covers nearly 100,000 acres in three counties, the watershed itself covers a bit less than 70,000 acres. Within this pear-shaped basin, at 3178 feet elevation, cold clear waters of Bull Run Lake seep through porous rock and drain into the Bull Run River. The river runs through the drainage, picking up additional water from tributaries, then flows into two reservoirs called creatively Bull Run Reservoir #1 and Bull Run Reservoir #2. Officials are considering construction of a third reservoir.

Portland officials pegged Bull Run as a possible water source way back in 1885. At that time, residents were drawing water from wells, the Willamette River, and local creeks. Portland was trying to shed its rustic "Stumptown" image and citizens realized they needed more reliable drinking water. City officials scouted the area and selected Bull Run watershed. Back then, they couldn't have known the wisdom of that choice.

In just the past ten years, researchers have recognized the unique qualities of old-growth Douglas-fir forests in capturing and purifying water. In addition, oriented as it is from east to west, Bull Run Watershed captures storm clouds as they roll in from the Pacific and traps them at its eastern end, wringing the moisture from them. This one watershed captures as much as 180 inches of precipitation annually, nearly twice that of watersheds to the north and south.

On June 17, 1892, President Benjamin Harrison proclaimed the Bull Run Watershed as a national forest reserve. Within a year, construction workers were running 24 miles of pipeline from the forest to the city. It is hard to imagine the labor involved in such a project, given the tools of the time. Meanwhile, reservoirs were built at high points in the city, one in Washington Park and one on Mt. Tabor, to provide local storage and a gravity feed.

On January 2, 1895, the first Bull Run River water flowed into Portland. The Portland Hotel's menu boasted that it served only Bull Run water to diners in its elegant restaurant. Within two years, health officials saw a phenomenal drop in cases of typhoid fever and the city death rate dropped to a record low.

To guard water purity, President Theodore Roosevelt signed the Trespass Act in 1904, prohibiting entry into the watershed except for official business. In 1912, timber tycoon Simon Benson donated brass four-bowl drinking fountains that still bubble Bull Run water throughout the Portland downtown area. The same year, Gresham began buying water from Portland. By 1929, the city constructed its first dam on the Bull Run River. A second dam was added in 1962 and other cities purchased Bull Run water for their citizens' use.

In 1958, the Forest Service reopened the area for "multiple use," including recreation and logging. The watershed was logged for over twenty years before a lawsuit forced Forest Service officials to rethink their management of the watershed. In 1977 the Management Unit designation was established into law. A 1996 law further restricted logging. Today, neither the logging trucks nor you are allowed in.

This is a large expanse of wild forest, and managers debate the value of intervention in nature's processes. The big concerns are wind, floods and fires. Wind storms blew down thousands of huge trees in 1931, and again in 1983. Floods in 1964 and 1996 caused massive damage and required round-the-clock repairs. There have been no large fires in the Bull Run since it became a regional water source. Experts estimate the watershed averages a big fire every 350 years. Most of today's big Doug firs sprouted after a huge hot fire in 1493.

Normally the moist watershed doesn't burn but given the right conditions—drought, lightning, and high winds—anything could happen.

Since 1972 the watershed has been jointly managed by the Forest Service and the Portland City Water Bureau. This joint-custody arrangement isn't without tensions. The Forest Service has difficulty retreating from a deeply ingrained legacy of timber cutting and still maintains that the watershed would be better managed with some logging. City officials are more closely tied to the shifting winds of local politics.

Somewhere in between lies the debate over proper management of wild lands that provide our most precious resource. Today, 25 percent of Oregonians get their water from the Bull Run Watershed and 40 percent of Oregonians get their water from Mt. Hood National Forest. A century ago, city officials with tremendous foresight established a lasting and pure water source. How we manage water quality and quantity will determine our survival in this century.

■ OTHER OPTIONS

For a long day hike, take the P.C.T. for four miles to the Lost Lake trail junction called Huckleberry Trail #617. Down a steep trail for just shy of two miles you find yourself on the road next to the lake.

Huckleberry foliage ignites the scree fields in autumn.

Lost Lake Shore

Trail #656

The Perfect Campsite

Recommended Season: Spring, Summer, Fall
Use: Heavy
Difficulty: Easy

MAPS

Mount Hood National Forest, Geo-Graphics Mt. Hood Wilderness, Green Trail #461 Government Camp.

DIRECTIONS

From Portland, take U.S. Highway 26 to Zigzag and turn left onto Lolo Pass Road, Forest Road 18. Follow this to Lolo Pass. Turn right onto McGee Creek Road, Forest Road 1810 and drive on gravel for seven miles. It rejoins Forest Road 18. After another seven miles, you'll come to a T intersection at Forest Road 13. Signs direct you from here. You'll turn left and take Road 13 to the lake.

From Hood River, take State Highway 35 to Woodworth Road. Turn right (west) and drive three miles to Dee Highway 281. Turn right (north) on 281, drive about five miles, make a very sharp left and cross the bridge. Stay left onto Lost Lake Road and follow signs to the lake.

Camping next to a lake is an ancient practice. Today, an ideal campsite offers easy access to water, a beautiful view, a flat place for a tent and a breeze to keep the bugs away. These are probably the same criteria local Indians used when choosing camp sites during summer berry picking season. Lost Lake is a near-perfect spot by these standards and has probably been used as a camp site for thousands of years.

Archaeologists recognize that Lost Lake has all the attributes of an ideal Indian camp site, yet have found very little evidence of Indian use here. The most likely explanation for the absence of artifacts is that campers today have their tents pitched on top of them. Lost Lake was developed as a campground so early that campsites were likely established right on top of the Indian sites. A well-established trail called the Walk Up Trail stretched from Sandy to The Dalles and passed near the lake and probably provided the route of the first road through the upper Hood River Valley and over Lolo Pass.

Old-growth grove of cedar and fir.

The Indians camped here while attending to serious business—gathering food. European Americans chose lakeside camping for different reasons. As Portland grew from a rough-and-tumble frontier town to a more sophisticated city, its residents longed to reconnect with the forest for adventure, rest, solitude and connection to nature. As far back as 1880, people headed to the mountains for vacations. Back then, there were no cars and it took a lot of determination to get to the woods. People came by steamboat and railcar to Hood River, then boarded the Mt. Hood Railroad to the small town of Dee. From there, they hiked, or later took horses or horse drawn carriages to Cloud Cap Inn at the foot of Elliot Glacier.

It was about that time that a group of twelve local citizens from Hood River, acting on a tip, scouted the area above Dee in search of a beautiful lake. When they finally found it they named it Lost Lake. Its postcard reflection of Mount Hood and its ideal camp sites made it a favorite early destination.

Camping caught on around the turn of the century as modes of transportation improved. The Forest Service started building official campgrounds. Lost Lake Campground was opened in 1900 and was one of the first Forest Service campgrounds in the country. To meet the demand for outdoor recreation, the agency built trails and roads into the most popular and scenic locations.

On a typical trip in the 1920s, a family would leave Union Station in Portland at 7:30 a.m., arrive in Hood River, then catch the train to Dee. A 1920s Forest Service brochure states, "From Dee the walk to the lake is 14 miles. Good camp grounds are situated about 7 miles from Dee on the Dee–Lost Lake Road. Vigorous hikers will make the trip to Lost Lake the same day. Automobile transportation may be secured for the trip from Dee to Cedar Springs, within 4 miles of the lake."

By the 1920s, many people in and around Portland had purchased automobiles and the demand for good roads became ever more intense. An American tradition, "car camping" was born. The

In this 1920s scene campers brought a bear rug and victrola.

Photo courtesy USDA Forest Service.

The view from Lost Lake is the classic postcard image of Mt. Hood.

Eagle Creek Campground in the Columbia River Gorge was the first Forest Service automobile campground, and served as a stopping point on the way to Dee and Lost Lake.

In the teens and twenties, families camped all summer. Often mother and children would set up camp and remain there for months at a time, while father would commute back and forth several times from Portland. Families set up camps that included full kitchens with wood-burning stoves. They baked bread and prepared complete meals. Going camping often meant bringing aunts, uncles, cousins—the entire extended family.

The original Lost Lake campground, located on the south shore, was abandoned and a new one built on the north. The campground is almost always filled in the summer, but as soon as school starts in the fall, crowds clear out and the forest colors up.

A 3.5-mile Lakeshore Trail follows the perimeter of the lake through old-growth forest. In the early 1990s, a one-mile barrier-free Old Growth Interpretive Trail was added. You can also head up to Lost Lake Butte from the general-store parking area. The trail is a steep two-miler that ends with views of the lake and Cascades peaks. As the Forest Service flyer says, "all it takes is an extra bowl of Wheaties."

If you choose to hike in, rather than drive, you can make a great day hike or backpack from Lolo Pass on the P.C.T. (Hike #6). The pleasant, moderately steep Huckleberry Trail #617 runs from the south end of Lost Lake to the P.C.T.

Little Zigzag Falls

Trail #795C

A Rest Stop on the Old Highway

Recommended Season: Summer and Fall
Difficulty: Easy

▨ MAP

Mount Hood National Forest.

▨ DIRECTIONS

From U.S. Highway 26, turn north on Kiwanis Camp Road #2639. Drive all the way to the end and park.

There is a wonderful little secret, just off U.S. Highway 26 between Government Camp and Rhododendron. If you find yourself driving over the pass on a hot summer day, dying for a break, take the Kiwanis Camp Road, Forest Road 2639, and follow it all the way to the end. There you will find a poorly-marked trailhead that leads to a natural refrigerator.

The sound of rushing water greets you as you enter the dense forest that shades this narrow canyon. The Little Zigzag River flows right off the glaciers above Little Zigzag Canyon and rushes past your feet. The river overflows its banks each spring, washing away the vegetation and leaving the forest floor next to the river nearly bare. Elsewhere shade and moisture-loving plants thrive. Rock benches provide a perch for views of the river and falls. Sit here for a while and tensions are bound to drift away.

Old highway railings provide clues to the past.

Oh, and what a delightfully refreshing sensation! Breezes through the canyon are warm one minute, then drop ten degrees to goose-bump cool. Even on a hot September afternoon, tiny ferns repelling from the perpendicular rock walls, dangle drops of water that catch gleams of light. Stroll an easy 1/4 mile to a tumbling waterfall. Late-summer runoff blasts through this canyon, so make sure the kids and grandma don't toddle too close to the water.

It isn't hard to imagine that this has long been a popular stop for families. Today, it has nearly been forgotten. Even when standing next to the falls, you hear the sound of Highway 26. Construction of that sleek, straightened, widened route around the mountain bypassed sections of an incredible scenic road built in 1924, and left to obscurity little cherished places like this.

Only remnants of the old highway remain. Didn't you pass some, when you left your car and walked to the trailhead? Did you see the old concrete railings? Mossy and cracked, they are some of the few remaining ruins of a highway that provided some of the first access to the forest and brought people in view of some of Oregon's most treasured scenery.

In 1910, there were few roads in Oregon. People traveled by boat, on foot, or by horse-drawn conveyance.

Trails, many dating back to presettlement Indian use, provided the connection between rural communities. But the automobile age had arrived, and these newfangled contraptions were showing up in Portland. People were recognizing the need for and value of good roads.

Through the efforts of a few visionaries and a number of wealthy businessmen, the first stretch of the Columbia River Highway was completed in 1913. One of the first paved roads in the Pacific Northwest, it connected Portland with Hood River through some of the nation's most exquisite scenery. It was so popular that people began to push for a connecting route around Mt. Hood.

People did drive from Sandy to Government Camp along a primitive single-lane road with turnouts. It was so deeply rutted that drivers got a workout trying to maintain control. In summer, people wore "dusters," light coats that would shield their clothing from the billowing clouds churned up by auto tires. In wet weather, cars sank to their hubs. Rocks and chuck holes would pitch cars so violently that springs would snap and tires would pop.

In 1915, a delegation of local officials including foresters, judges,

Little Zigzag Falls roars over boulders and logs.

business people, and an *Oregon Journal* reporter scouted potential routes around the mountain. Traveling on horseback, they camped at Elk Meadow, then explored routes down to Newton Creek, and up the East Fork of Hood River to Bennett Pass, White River, the Barlow Summit, and into Summit Meadow and Government Camp. The trip made enthusiastic supporters of them all.

Much of the work to build the road was done by hand and with horse-drawn teams, as heavy road construction machinery didn't yet exist. Construction was limited to a short season. The section between Government Camp and Horsethief Meadow wasn't completed until 1924, as work couldn't begin until July and ended by October.

In the 1920s, the route offered a wide array of dining and hotel accommodations. Road houses were a favorite feature of the Columbia River route, serving hot meals to weary tourists. Motorists could check into Hood River area hotels, or head toward the mountain. Mt. Hood Lodge offered a spectacular view of the mountain. More adventuresome travelers could chug six

The Little Zigzag River chills this small canyon.

miles off the highway to the 6000-foot level and stay at Cloud Cap Inn, at the base of Elliot Glacier. The Government Camp Hotel, the Arrah Wanna Hotel and a number of taverns dotted the south side of the route.

For many people, the new highway offered them their first view of the east side of Mt. Hood. Captivated by new-found freedom, people headed to the forest in their wheezing and banging conveyances. The Mt. Hood Loop was touted as "destined to become the greatest motor drive in America" with the potential to make Portland "what it naturally should be—the tourist center of the Pacific Northwest." In 1926, Secretary of Agriculture W.M. Jardine established the Mt. Hood Recreation Area, which included the national forest lands adjacent to the highway.

The original Mt. Hood Loop circling the mountain from Gresham to Hood River was a meandering highway, dotted with bridges that crossed Mt.

Photo courtesy USDA Forest Service.

1920s tourists enjoy the Mt. Hood Loop.

Hood's many creeks. But inevitably traffic increased on the highway, and people wanted to go faster. Over the years, the highway was "improved," straightened and rerouted to facilitate swift travel in all seasons.

And so, these old railings sit abandoned and a bit forlorn. Mosses creep across their stained surfaces. Each season's ice and snow widens small fissures and gradually crumbles them. But still they stand, having witnessed the first motorists to climb this mountain route. You can almost hear the laughter, the chugging and banging of a Model A, the squeals of excitement at each new vista. Oh, what a time it must have been!

Look for other remnants of the old road. A stretch of the old highway runs around the base of Laurel Hill and ends at a waterfall. You can also feel the old road by driving to the Glacier View Sno-park across from Mt. Hood Ski Bowl. The sno-park is part of the old highway. By crossing Highway 26 into the Ski Bowl parking lot, driving through the lot, then crossing again and driving through Government Camp, you experience the graceful curves of the old highway and see the slash that Highway 26 made through it. You can visit other sections of the original highway at Sahalie Falls and near Pioneer Woman's Grave. That section of the Barlow Road #3531 became part of the Mt. Hood Loop. The old stone water fountains can be seen at both of these sites.

■ CONNECTING TRAILS

From the trailhead, walk between the railings and up the old road. In a short distance, you'll reach an overpass above the Old Pioneer Bridle Trail. Scramble down to it and head east to Enid Lake or west to Laurel Hill. This stretch between Enid and the Kiwanis Camp follows the Barlow Road.

Mirror Lake

Trail #664
Popular To A Fault

Recommended Seasons: Spring, Summer and Fall
Use: Extremely heavy
Difficulty: Easy

MAPS

Mount Hood National Forest, Geo-Graphics Mt. Hood Wilderness

DIRECTIONS

Mirror Lake trailhead is one mile west of Government Camp. It is easy to find. There are always a slew of cars lined up at the trailhead on the south side of U.S. Highway 26.

Mirror Lake is one of those little gems within Mt. Hood National Forest and no hiking guide to this forest would be complete without it. It is a mountain lake that usually reflects a perfect image of Mt. Hood. The trail begins on a rustic bridge, crossing a picturesque water fall, then providing an easy 1 1/2-mile stroll from a trailhead that sits smack dab on one of the most heavily traveled stretches of U.S. Highway 26, in the heart of the recreation corridor.

When I talked to one of my Forest Service buddies about downplaying this trail to discourage use, he couldn't quite bring himself to be as critical of Mirror Lake as I. "I had a nice time with my family there last weekend. It wasn't all that crowded." Mind you, I had stopped at the trailhead that same September Sunday and counted 44 cars.

There's no doubt about it, people are willing to share this special place with dozens of others because they love it. And there lies the problem. Mirror Lake tempts you with easy access to scenery that you usually see on magazine covers. By doing so it draws thousands of people every year to a place that can't handle thousands of people.

The lake itself is much smaller than you might think, judging by its reputation and the number of cars at the trailhead. Its eastern shores are heavily trampled and there are toilet-paper flags in many of the bushes. The wetland on the south shore was granted a bit of a reprieve from foot traffic with construction of a wooden boardwalk, but now people are camping in the reeds and building fires in it. The western shore is bounded by large stones and that is where the designated camp sites are located.

Trail #664 continues past the west side of the lake and heads up to the three peaks of Tom Dick and Harry Mountain to the south. It crosses the slope above U.S. 26, providing a sweeping view of this travel corridor and its mountain towns nestled below Mt. Hood. Huckleberries ripen across this slope in August, and glow with red foliage in September. The rocky top of Harry is home to pikas and marmots and provides views of several Cascades peaks. Tom and Dick are closed to protect peregrine falcon habitat. An older

Mirror Lake proves that it was aptly named.

abandoned trail from Multorpor Ski Area used to skirt the side of Tom, ending at Wind Lake to the south.

My guess is that most people who come here remain at Mirror Lake. It gives people what they seek in a day hike. Mt. Hood is an urban forest, meaning that it is located within an easy drive from a large metropolitan area that has adopted this forest as its playground. With this proximity to a million and a half people looking for a nice place to spend Sunday afternoon, some places in the forest will draw crowds and suffer for it.

Mirror Lake sits outside designated wilderness. This makes it easier for the Forest Service to build some facilities to better manage the crowds. Restroom facilities and a few more shoreline structures would do a lot to prevent further damage. On the other hand, many of Mt. Hood's most beloved places are

located within Mt. Hood Wilderness where facilities are supposed to be primitive, in keeping with the natural surroundings. It should be expected that people are going to flock to spots like Ramona Falls and Cairn Basin that offer magnificent scenery and are accessible only a few months out of the year. Realistically, these are not places to seek wilderness solitude.

I happen to love solitary hikes and avoid places that are crowded or trampled. While Mt. Hood is heavily used for recreation by its urban constituents, it provides surprisingly easy access to solitude. You may notice that most of the photos in this book have no people in them. That's not because I told people to get out of the way when I shot the pictures, but because I was totally alone on many of these hikes.

I do expect that sites with exquisite scenery, easy access, and proximity to the mountain will be crowded. This eight-acre pool bordered by forest and reflecting that perfect mirror image of our favorite mountain is genuinely soothing to the soul. And the trail is wide and easy. And perhaps many of the folks who come here enjoy being in the company of others who are also enjoying this scene.

Rather than discourage you from going there, I suggest you treat this little mountain lake gently, pick up your own trash and the trash left by others, and stay on hard surfaces or established trails to avoid trampling vegetation and eroding the shoreline. I don't recommend camping here. Consider trying other lakes that are a bit quieter or have been developed for use by lots of people. Here are some suggestions, all within an easy Sunday afternoon drive:

■ LESS PERFECT BUT QUIETER SMALL LAKES

Catalpa Lake: Trail #535. Take U.S. 26 to Highway 35 to Forest Road 48 to 43 to 43-250.

Boulder Lake and Little Boulder Lake: See Hike #17.

Bear Lake and Rainy Lake: From Hood River, take 13th Street south and follow signs to Odell for 3.4 miles. After the Hood River Bridge, turn right, go past Tucker Park. In 6.3 miles veer right toward Dee, cross the river and turn right following signs to Rainy Lake, first on paved Punchbowl Road, then Forest Road 2820 to the trailhead.

■ EASY-ACCESS LAKES THAT MIRROR MT. HOOD

Trillium Lake: See Hike #10.

Lost Lake: See Hike #7.

Timothy Lake: See Hike #25.

Frog Lake: U.S. 26 just past Wapanitia Pass, turn east on Forest Road 2610.

Mt. Hood and Mirror Lake from Harry Mountain.

Veda Lake

Trail #673

Fish in the Clouds

Recommended Seasons: Spring, Summer and Fall
Use: Medium
Difficulty: Moderate

MAPS

Mount Hood National Forest, Geo-Graphics Mount Hood Wilderness, Green Trails Map #461 Government Camp and #462 Mt. Hood.

DIRECTIONS

Take U.S. Highway 26 east of the summit and watch for signs to Still Creek Campground. Drive through Still Creek Campground, continue for one mile to the second road to the right called East Chimney Rock Road. Follow this for 1/2 mile to a four-way intersection. Continue south on Sherar Burn Road 2613 for 3 1/2 miles on rough rocky one-lane road to Fir Tree Campground and Veda Lake Trailhead. Call Mt. Hood Information Center for road conditions.

Veda Lake is nestled on the north side of the long ridge that separates the Still Creek and Salmon River watersheds. The road to the trailhead is a nasty three-and-a-half-mile bounce over pointed boulders and through axle-cracking ruts. In fact, the road to the trailhead is much more challenging than the hike. If your rig can tolerate the abuse, you're rewarded with a pleasant mile-long stroll up and over the ridge. From your ridge-top vantage point, Mt. Hood lounges in full view on the other side of the Still Creek drainage, and you'll catch a bird's eye preview of the gleaming lake below.

On hot summer days, Veda beckons panting hikers to swim and munch M&Ms in the shade for the remainder of the afternoon. Wool-clad autumn hikers reap colorful rewards from lipstick-red vine maple and huckleberry in openings along the ridge and around the lake shore.

Veda is also an attractive lake for those who can't resist a pan full of sizzling, freshly-caught trout. Choose to fish here and you'll join a long tradition of avid anglers who have come to mountain lakes for the challenge, tranquility and solitude. Most high-mountain lakes have cold, very pure water. That purity seems like it would provide pristine conditions for fish but in fact, it can be a negative for fish survival. A lack of minerals and a short growing season make high cold lakes low in nutrients that the fish need to thrive. Many don't support native populations of fish, or they were fished-out soon after their "discovery" by recreational anglers.

As westerners became more mobile in the 1910s and 20s, they sought more outdoor recreation and in an effort to meet their needs, Oregon's Department of Fish and Game (now called Fish and Wildlife) stocked mountain lakes and streams with favorite frying-pan fish. Often the choice of fish was based on what tasted good or provided good sport, not what might be native to the lake.

Veda was named for Vern Rogers and Dave Donaldson who packed into the lake in 1917 with the lake's first load of baby trout. George Ledford, the local forest ranger, created the name "Veda" by combining the first two letters from Vern and Dave. These men had their work cut out for them, as the legal limit back then was 100 fish!

Veda is still stocked today with eastern brook trout. Every two years, Oregon Department of Fish and Wildlife sends out a helicopter with a load of baby brookies destined for Veda Lake. The last time anyone from O.D.F.W. checked on what was living in Veda Lake was 1964. Using a gill net, biologists swept the lake and checked the net's contents.

Across the west, researchers are beginning to evaluate the effects of nearly 100 years of stocking fishless high-elevation lakes with nonnative fish. The bulk of this research was initiated in just the last ten years. In California, biologists and conservationists are concerned that the tradition of stocking high Sierra lakes may have had serious consequences for the salamanders, frogs, insects and other creatures that normally live in this cold pure water habitat. Additional research is focused on the North Cascades in Washington.

Even when they contain the same species, high lakes vary from one to the next. The structure of the lake—its depth, size, shape, rocks and vegetation—create a unique environment in which the living creatures in the lake organize themselves. The dissolved minerals and other nutrients in its water and the length of time it remains under ice also determine what lives there. In

most cases, organisms adapted to each lake's environment and to each other over thousands of years. In this environment, amphibians top the food chain, feeding on insects and algae.

From recent studies, it appears that frog and salamander populations are significantly lower in stocked lakes, perhaps because the fish and amphibians compete for the same food. In the North Cascades, researchers observed salamanders swimming freely in the fishless lakes, and basking openly on logs and rocks. In the stocked lakes, salamanders were more secretive, hiding in crevices of submerged boulders and probably feeding at night. Fish had salamander larvae in their stomachs.

Researchers know that baby fish eat differently than adult fish. Adult fish eat larger food, while small fry eat smaller food. An introduction of baby fish once every two years may send populations of plankton and other tiny plants and animals crashing. In addition, as fish mature and eat greater numbers of large insects, these insects eat less of the algae and microorganisms. All of this alters the relationships of the insects and other organisms that affect the nutrient balance in the lake water.

Nobody knows if these same concerns are valid at Veda Lake, because no one from Fish and Wildlife checks. With 55 biologists statewide to keep track of thousands of these little lakes, there aren't enough people to go out and check each lake. Like Veda, many lakes haven't been checked since Lyndon Johnson was president.

From the shore, Veda Lake still appears tranquil and beautiful. It is hard to imagine life-and-death struggles

Hikers are rewarded with this first view of Veda Lake.

going on just under the surface. The family I met at the trailhead begged me not to put their favorite little hideaway in this book. Sorry folks, here it is. Many of us have special places in the forest that we would love to keep secret. Visit Veda on a weekday or off-season weekend and it will still feel like your secret little spot. Ever since Vern and Dave, people have hiked to this pretty little lake to enjoy the smell of fir trees and forest duff on a warm summer day and to watch little rings echo to the shore after a fish leaps to chase a bug.

Grandparents guide a young angler at Trillium Lake.

▓ TRILLIUM LAKE

Trillium Lake is another mountain lake worthy of a visit. It too is a favorite destination for families of anglers and is stocked annually with brook and rainbow trout. Trillium Lake Loop Trail #761 circles the lake, with elevated boardwalks providing dry passage over the wetland shoreline. From the south side of the lake, enjoy postcard-quality views of Mt. Hood. Trillium is a 57-acre reservoir created when Mud Creek was dammed. Summit Meadows, north of the lake, provides an indication of what the area was like prior to the dam. Summit meadows blooms throughout the summer with a rich array of wildflowers including gentian, spirea, lupine and orchids. An interpretive sign in the meadow describes the relief felt by Oregon Trail emigrant's who arrived at the meadow with famished animals. Nearby, a picket fence surrounds the graves of Perry Vickers, Baby Barclay, Baby Morgan and an unknown woman, all casualties of the arduous "Great Migration" along the Oregon Trail. This area is open for hiking from May to October and makes a great Nordic ski destination in the winter.

Photo by Tom Iraci.

On a calm day the view across Trillium Lake is unsurpassed.

Timberline Trail

Trail #600

The Trail to Paradise, The Rainshadow
Scoured by Glaciers

Recommended Seasons: Summer, Fall
Use: Heavy
Difficulty: Strenuous

MAPS

Mount Hood National Forest, Geo-Graphics Mount Hood Wilderness, Green Trails Mt. Hood #462 and, U.S.G.S. Mt. Hood North and, Forest Service brochure Timberline Trail #600—a brief guide.

If you were to choose a single trail on which to see the wonders of this stretch of the Cascades, and you visited nothing else in Mt. Hood National Forest, the trail to choose would be the Timberline Trail. It is a beautifully constructed and maintained passage to sweeping vistas, physical challenge, and spiritual calm. The trail takes you through valleys of glacial grit and volcanic ash blown from the mountain's past eruptions. You'll walk among glacier lilies or wade through hip-deep lupine in wildflower meadows so exquisite, they will break your heart. And from points around the mountain you'll view an expanse of the Pacific Northwest that includes eastern sagebrush country; Portland

and the Coast Range; and as many as seven major Cascade peaks from Mt. Rainier to the north, to the Three Sisters to the south.

Lodges and shelters along the Timberline Trail have welcomed guests for generations. On the northeast side of the mountain, Cloud Cap Inn has sent a warm glow across the rocky windswept bluffs since 1889 and regal Timberline Lodge welcomed its first guests in 1937. Seven small stone huts are anchored to the mountain at strategic spots, constructed as a courtesy to weary hikers by the depression-era Civilian Conservation Corps.

View along Timberline Trail.

Photo by John Tullis.

Lush wildflower meadows in Cairn Basin.

backpacking trip, spread over three or more days. A few ultra-distance runners circle the mountain in an arduous single workout. However, the trail is ideally constructed for those who can spare only a day at a time. More than a dozen trails intersect the Timberline Trail from all sides of the mountain, like roads to a roundabout. Using a car shuttle or exchange, you can enjoy sections of the trail over a series of weekend day hikes.

▌ TIMBERLINE LODGE TO LOLO PASS

The Trail to Paradise

Most hikers setting off on the Timberline Trail begin their adventure at Timberline Lodge. The elegant mountain lodge was built by the Works Progress Administration, a depression-era program that put unemployed men to work on projects focused on the arts.

While the scenic splendor along this trail is often grand in scale, many of its most enchanting scenes are in miniature. Springs and seeps send droplets dancing through a grotto of tiny ferns. Yellow monkey flowers wave to royal blue gentians on the opposite shore of a splashing brook. Butterflies dance atop pearly everlasting and yarrow. Sun-burnished sedums huddle in crevices below rock outcrops splotched like a painter's palette with chartreuse and storm-cloud-gray lichens.

If you choose to circle the entire mountain in one trip, you will hike 40.7 miles, with about 9000 feet of elevation gained and lost as you cross through glacier-fed river canyons. It is a popular

The trail was part of a larger plan to provide public access to the timberline area of the mountain, while preserving its beautiful and fragile alpine environment.

While the Timberline Trail formally connected older established trails, it was planned, designed, and built as a complete trail system, with shelters strategically placed every four miles or so. Built by Civilian Conservation Corps craftsmen, most of the work was done in the summer of 1934, with the Yocum Ridge section completed the following year.

When the trail was proposed, access to the mountain was very limited. There was a trail from the Mt. Hood Loop Highway to Paradise Park, a trail up Vista Ridge to Eden Park, a road to Cloud Cap, and a climbers' trail from Government Camp to the mountain's summit.

Mountain recreation was rapidly gaining popularity and developers saw the potential to cash in on it. In 1927, the Cascade Development Company of Portland proposed a resort hotel at Cloud Cap and a tramway to the summit. There was so much public controversy over this proposal that the Forest Service sought help, consulting some of the best minds in the country, including Landscape Architect Fredrick Law Olmstead who designed Central Park in New York City, and John Merriam, President of the Carnegie Institute. Based on their advice and extensive field work, the Forest Service developed a comprehensive recreation plan that included motor vehicle access, trails, campgrounds, and a resort lodge on the mountain's south side. Most of the plan was designed by agency recreation planner Francis Williamson, Jr. based at Zigzag Ranger Station.

Completed in 1930, it was the first plan brought to Congress for funding that was purely for recreational development. Complementing and complicating the recreation plan, the chief of the Forest Service designated Mt. Hood as a Primitive Area, an entirely new designation and the precursor to wilderness status. Congress, struggling with the country's economic depression, denied the request for funding.

But when Franklin Roosevelt took office in 1932 and started programs to help unemployed workers, the Forest Service had plans in hand to put men to work. The Civilian Conservation Corps went to work on the Timberline Trail in 1933. They also constructed the road to Timberline Lodge.

Few changes have been made to the trail route over the years. The Timberline Lodge trailhead was moved because the area around the lodge was getting badly trampled. The section north of Yocum Ridge was raised to a higher point on the mountain to improve the views. The junction with Ramona Falls Trail was modified after the Sandy River decided to change its course. Construction of Mount Hood Meadows Ski Area significantly changed the scenery for trail users through that stretch.

Other than these changes, the trail has remained as it was built in 1934. The charming little shelters have taken abuse over the years from the intense winter weather that hammers the mountain at this elevation. The Elk Cove shelter was destroyed by an avalanche in 1948. The Gnarl Ridge structure collapsed under heavy snow load. The shelter near Mt. Hood Meadows built just off the trail, likely was never used much. Today it is a ruin which you can't see from the trail.

If you start this historic trail headed west from Timberline Lodge, you'll hike the section where the Pacific Crest National Scenic Trail and the Timberline Trail come together as one. The trail passes through Paradise Park, one of the mountain's most exquisite wildflower extravaganzas. Here the Paradise Loop Trail offers more expanded exploration of the expanses of swaying fragrant flowers that bloom from snow melt to snow fall. There are two significant river crossings on this section, one at

Zigzag Canyon and the other at the Sandy River which is the lowest point on the trail. You can hop off the trail to view Ramona Falls.

TIMBERLINE LODGE

Timberline Lodge is an elegant stately structure, welcoming tired travelers and chilly skiers into its warm embrace. Built in the midst of the severe economic depression of the 1930s, it displays the craftsmanship and artistry of workers recruited under Franklin Roosevelt's Works Progress Administration, an employment program focused on art,

Timberline Lodge.

music and literature. It was the largest recreation project initiated under the W.P.A. and the first government-owned hotel in a national forest.

Using regional art and building techniques, the lodge was intended to encourage Oregonians' sense of identity in a time of economic despair. Its architects established a distinctly American alpine theme called "Cascadian," using

boulders in exterior walls and giant columns representing old-growth trees. You can find its most distinctive feature, the "Timberline arch," a squared cross beam with curved supports and corner brackets, in the main entrance, interior windows and even furniture. Regional art is featured throughout, repeating themes of nature, American Indians, and pioneer life.

The elegant old lodge is a great stop before or after hiking the Timberline Trail. Stop by for a tour, enjoy a meal, or spend the night in one of its cozy rustic rooms.

LOLO PASS TO CLOUD CAP

The Rain Shadow

The Cascade rain shadow is enormous, effectively slicing Oregon into two radically different climate zones. The divide is stark, startling, and surreal. Sallie Tisdale wrote of this sharp divide in *Stepping Westward*, "At every pass up and down the length of the Cascades, on every ridge where the pines stand up like bristles on a toothbrush, is a border. The soil changes, the trees and rocks change, the sky and the temperature and the light change. The transition is both reliable and abrupt. Sagebrush and scattered Ponderosa replace hemlock and vine maple."

There is no better place to see this in bold relief than by hiking the Timberline Trail. The west side of the trail traces the uppermost reaches of a dense wet forest, traversing lush wildflower meadows. Dozens of creeks, springs and rivers drain the massive melting snow pack from the mountain. But by the time you circle north and reach Cooper Spur, you've hit a transition zone. The north side of the mountain stays colder and loses snow later.

Plants here cling to rocks in an austere environment where glaring sun beams off the glaciers and their sandy moraines. Water sources are fewer across the eastern stretch of trail and views open to the east across pine oak savannah to rolling eastern Oregon fields.

Mt. Hood towers over the surrounding Cascades and acts as an impediment to eastbound clouds blowing from the Pacific Ocean. Gathering moisture on their journey over the ocean, wet Pacific storm clouds travel inland and bump up against the western slopes of the mountain. The air is forced upward, it cools, and its load of moisture condenses as rain or snow. By the time these clouds have passed the mountain, they have lost most of their oomph. This side of Mt. Hood averages 85 inches of precipitation each year, compared to the east side average of 20 inches.

If latitude alone decided weather, northern Oregon should have the same weather as Duluth, Minnesota; Newfoundland; or Mongolia. But West Coast weather systems, blowing off the Pacific ocean, are tempered by the largest body of water on the planet. We just don't build up the chill that accumulates in the middle of a land mass. Cold air tends to be dryer, while warmer air carries lots of moisture. We are blessed with temperate moisture.

Mild as our climate tends to be generally, the mountain's weather is unpredictable. The first year I hiked the trail in preparation for this book, it was a lovely day in late July. Clouds rolled in by late morning and before long we were surrounded, like being wrapped in a big white wet blanket.

At this elevation on a Cascades peak you have to be prepared for anything. In the middle of August, in 85-degree air under clear blue skies, even with a forecast of high pressure and clear weather, be ready to bundle up in fleece or wool and waterproof gear. Hypothermia is a serious concern here. Conditions change in minutes. Winds whipping against clammy skin and damp cotton clothes can send your body temperature plummeting, especially when you get tired or when a hard hike leaves you a bit dehydrated.

As an example, the next year, back on the Timberline Trail in the third week in August, we were delighted with a breezy warm day and an exquisite wildflower show. Rains had ceased in late June and while the Willamette Valley was parched beyond anything I can recall in the past twenty years, the mountain had collected a good snow pack over the winter, and the upper slopes were still moist, the wildflowers were lush.

Splashes of color along Timberline Trail.

Lupine meadows and Mt. Hood views make this a hiker's paradise.

But the following week, rain came early to the valley. And snow levels in the mountains dropped to 5,000 feet. "Unseasonably cool" the weather folk said. Warnings went out to campers and backpackers to carry appropriate clothing and plan for cold temperatures. I could hardly imagine my meadows of lupine, valerian and asters buried under a soggy dumping of snow.

Most years, snow remains on the mountain down to about 4000 feet until at least June. The Timberline Trail is usually passable by mid July, although this varies from year to year. Snow sometimes returns by September. It has such a short season, I tend to tolerate, even welcome, more people than I might normally hope to see on the trail. Popular areas feel almost like a city park on a summer weekend, but I've found that here there is a communion, an easy rapport with fellow hikers, perhaps a shared sense that we are in the presence of something spectacular, fragile and fleeting.

McGee Creek Trail #627 and Top Spur Trail #784A are both great places to hop on the Timberline Trail from the west side.

■ CLOUD CAP TO TIMBERLINE LODGE

Scoured by Glaciers

Mt. Hood gained its bold stature through a series of volcanic eruptions. But it got its appearance from slow rivers of ice that carve its rugged good looks. Eleven glaciers gradually pulverize the surface of the mountain, defining its ridges and deepening its river canyons. Elliot, Newton Clark, White River, Palmer, Zigzag, Reid, Sandy, Glisan, Ladd, Coe, and Langille glaciers grind away at the mountain. Joining forces with frost action, running water and wind, they've worn away almost 800 feet of its height.

The grinding power of these ice sheets, and more precisely the boulders and rock fragments imbedded in them, is most obvious along White, Sandy, and Zigzag rivers whose beds and banks are gray expanses of course gravel and gritty volcanic sand. In the late summer, when clear snow melt is exhausted, the glaciers themselves begin to melt and the water turns milky with suspended rock dust, called glacial flour. White River got its name from this milky appearance.

Glacier-fed streams and rivers around Mt. Hood fluctuate wildly over the summer season. The west side of the mountain accumulates so much snow that the late-spring and early- summer runoff comes in torrents, blasting through creeks and river valleys. Runoff tends to be more steady through July and August when dry weather prevails. But if warm rain hits the mountain snows in late spring or early fall, or we get a blast of hot weather, the mountain is prone to glacial outbursts.

Glacial outburst floods, or jöökulhlaups (an Icelandic term pronounced Yo-kul-hloips) become lahars or debris flows when they pick up rocks, sand and gravel. A lahar is like a six-foot-deep slurry of wet cement traveling at 20 miles per hour down the river channel. In recent years, White River has been especially prone to them, making it a challenge for both hikers and motorists. The White River crossing on the Timberline Trail is closed from time to time when conditions are dangerous. The bridge over White River on State Highway 35 is frequently damaged by volkswagen-sized-boulders carrie downstream by the power of these floods.

Outburst floods are unpredictable and dangerous. During hot or rainy weather, if you are near a stream and hear a roaring sound from above or see a rapid rise in water, immediately get away from the stream to higher ground.

River crossings on the Timberline Trail pose its greatest challenges. On some rivers, temporary bridges are helicoptered in each July and removed in October. But these rivers change course seasonally over a quarter-of-a-mile channel, making bridging difficult. It is common for bridges around the mountain to blow out during storms or hot spells. Hikers should use great caution, and when possible, cross first thing in the morning, when the rivers are at their lowest flow.

White River and Newton Creek both provide vivid views of glacier-fed rivers. You can hop on this stretch of the trail from Cooper Spur, Elk Meadows Trail (Hike #13), Heather Canyon (Hike #14) or Umbrella Falls Trail #667.

MOUNT HOOD EAST
White River and
Hood River Watersheds

Grave Trail

Trail #668

The Barlow Road Section of the Old Oregon Trail

Recommended Seasons: Spring, Summer and Fall
Use: Vary
Difficulty: Easy

▎MAPS

Mount Hood National Forest, Geo-Graphics Mt. Hood Wilderness Map, The Barlow Road brochure and map.

▎DIRECTIONS

From U.S. Highway 26 take State Highway 35 north and watch immediately for signs to Pioneer Woman's Grave. Turn south at Forest Road 3531 follow it approximately 2 miles. The site is well marked. Park just beyond the grave. The trail begins on the opposite side of the road. You can also start at Barlow Pass SnoPark and walk down to Road 3531.

If you want to get a real taste of what it felt like to be a pioneer on the old Oregon Trail, come to this site on a cold, rainy autumn day and walk this trail. By the time many emigrants reached this section of the trail it was late fall. They had traveled for over six months, their clothes were threadbare, their shoes were worn through and many of them were ill. The weather had turned wet and cold and they were in a race to get over the pass before snow trapped them here.

In any weather, Pioneer Woman's Grave is a poignant spot. The rock mound that marks the grave is usually dotted with flowers and small mementos. People are clearly touched by the tragic irony of a woman surviving the hardships of the Oregon Trail journey, only to die here in the mountains, a few miles from her destination. In 1924, road construction crews building the Mt. Hood Loop Highway discovered her body and moved her remains to the side of the road.

From this spot you can reach two sections of the Barlow Road, displaying some of the best original wagon ruts. This is a great spot for "rut nuts," those of us who are captivated by the fact that 150 years after they passed, you can still see the tracks from thousands of Oregon Trail wagons. Here the ruts are clearly visible, and across the road, the Grave Trail #668 connects the grave site with Barlow Pass.

On this one-mile stretch of the Barlow Road, look for other signs left by the thousands of people who passed through here in the "Great Migration" between 1845 and 1857. With a keen eye, you will find rope-burned trees where pioneers tied their wagons to the trees and inched them down the hill. You can find engravings in the trees. Some are initials, some are mileage numbers telling those who follow how far they must go to reach their destination in Oregon City. Signs of more recent activities can be seen here, too. Look for wooden pegs that held the first telephone lines stretching over the pass to remote Forest Service cabins. Three small holes in one tree reveal where a mountain trapper hung his snares for martens.

Immediately west of Pioneer Woman's Grave, wagon trains forded the east fork of the Salmon River. Emigrants picked rocks from the road and pitched them aside creating rock walls on either side and a trench almost five feet deep. On the embankment to the right, drop down into the trees. Here you will find some of the best-preserved wagon ruts in Mt. Hood National Forest, the result of thousands of feet, hooves and wagon wheels pounding the ground.

Listen. Can you hear the soft jingle of bridles, the squeak of leather harness and the creaking of wooden wagon frames? How many exhausted people and animals passed through here? What were folks thinking as they placed one tired foot down after the other, and strained to pull weary animals and worn wagons over never-ending logs and rocks.

The opening of Oregon Country for settlement began in 1843. Settlers gathered in Independence, Missouri, purchased and packed the last of their supplies and hit the trail when weather permitted, usually in May. Often groups of newly-aquainted settlers formed wagon trains, providing a greater sense of community and safety on the long journey. Their journey took them across deserts, mountains, through blowing dust and treacherous river crossings.

By the time they arrived at the Columbia River near The Dalles, after months of hardship, they were faced with a difficult choice. They could load their wagons on rafts and float the wild rapids of the mighty Columbia, or they could climb over the Cascade Mountains around the south side of Mt. Hood.

Pioneers must have had mixed feelings as they gazed at Mount Hood. Struck by the beauty of the mountain, they also knew they had to get around this last great barrier.

You can make Oregon history come

Wagons were lowered by rope down rocky Laurel Hill.

alive with an autumn car camping weekend traveling the Barlow Road. The trail runs across the entire forest, from the eastern boundary at the Rock Creek Reservoir in Tygh Valley, to the Tollgate Campground near the western forest boundary. In late September and early October, the oaks in Tygh Valley turn crimson, russet and gold. Back-lit vine maples illuminate the entire stretch from Gate Creek to Tollgate.

You'll find that the pioneer experi-

ence becomes very real when you walk a stretch of the old route, stopping to read passages from a pioneer journal. During the 150-year Oregon Trail anniversary celebration in 1993, lots of pioneer journals, brochures and maps were published and interpretive signs were placed at key sites. Forest information centers even stock wagon packing lists and dutch-oven recipes. Highway markers provide good directions to important or well-preserved spots.

Thirty miles of the original route are still "intact." Unfortunately, most of the stretch on the west side of the mountains is now beneath U.S. Highway 26. You can follow some of what remains there on the Pioneer Bridle Trail between Enid Lake and Tollgate Campground.

The best part is a 23-mile stretch from Gate Creek to Barlow Pass. It is maintained as a primitive dirt road which means during the dry season you can drive much of it and bike all of it. There is a rough section east of Forest Creek Campground, and the road conditions do change each year, so check with the Mt. Hood Information Center or Barlow Ranger District for the latest report. They sell the Barlow Road map which is packed with information. You can use the forest recreation map and follow the route of Road 3530. Some of the best sites include Faith, Hope and Charity Springs, White River Station, Fort Deposit, Devil's Half Acre, Summit Meadows, Laurel Hill, and Tollgate Replica.

Happy rut hunting!

Follow the wagon ruts made by pioneers long ago.

13

Elk Meadows Loop

Trails #645, #652, #600, #646

A Subalpine Parkland

Recommended Seasons: Summer and Fall
Use: Medium
Difficulty: Strenuous

■ MAPS

Mount Hood National Forest, Geo-Graphics Mt. Hood Wilderness.

■ DIRECTIONS

Drive east on Highway 26 to the junction for Highway 35. Take 35 north and follow signs to Hood River Meadows. Just past the Hood River Meadows turnoff, watch for signs for Clark Creek Sno-Park. Drive through the sno-park to Elk Meadows trailhead.

The trail to Elk Meadows requires wet feet and courage. If you love river crossings, this is the place for you. Bridges aren't very practical in a landscape where creeks and rivers turn to torrents every spring. So hikers pick their way through boulders and dip warm toes into newly-thawed water so cold it hurts. But the rewards for braving these crossings and panting up the hill are worth it—waving grass, bog orchids, and Mt. Hood in your lap.

Elk Meadow is the largest meadow on the mountain. On Mt. Hood's eastern flank, between glacier-cut ridges and gritty river valleys, the landscape is softened by an expansive carpet of moist flowery grassland. In contrast to the rugged subalpine ridges above, these meadows on gentler slopes hold moisture through the summer.

This open country that delights us in summer appeals to ski resort developers, too. On winter weekends, nearby Mt. Hood Meadows, Heather Canyon, and Hood River Meadows attract thousands of nordic and alpine skiers. But these places weren't named while they were under snow. When the deep snow fields that challenge skiers melt in the spring sun, the frozen ground below awakens. Delicate white avalanche lilies are among the first brave pioneers to appear along the edges of snow banks. By mid July, only a glint of snow remains in the shade and the meadows come out of winter dormancy with a burst of fresh growth and dazzling color.

In its short snow-free season, Elk Meadow provides habitat for an interesting variety of wetland and bog plants. In early August, the green expanse of sedges is highlighted with white spires of bog orchids. Also called bog candles, their stalks grow to three feet tall, standing head and shoulder above the grassy meadow growth. Each is a long dense cluster of small blooms.

Oregon is home to several exquisite wild orchids. Orchids are pollinated by insects, and many have developed interesting means for convincing their polli-

Bog orchids bloom in Mt. Hood's largest meadow.

nators to transport the goods. Bog orchids hide their nectar behind each fragrant white bloom up and down their stems, and they powder their stems with pollen. Only pollinators with long flexible tongues, usually moths, are rewarded with nectar. As the moth reaches its tongue way down behind the flower to reach the nectar, it bumps its forehead into the flower's pollen-coated stem. It then carries its little powdered head to the next orchid.

A small rustic shelter adds to Elk Meadow's charm.

Magenta elephanthead share a liking for Elk Meadows, along with lupine, valerian and arrowleaf groundsel. The meadow provides habitat for a variety of birds and mammals. As the name implies, elk find high-elevation meadows to their liking during summer months, retreating to lower-elevation forests in winter.

Just a mile above the meadow, there is a shift to steeper country where moisture drains quickly when snows melt and thin sandy soils turn dry and dusty. Clumps of gnarled trees cling to rock outcrops and dry meadows of bicolor lupine and aster endure the late summer drought.

This is what most people would call "timberline." In fact this term describes more of a zone than a line. In general, mountain forests are called "montane." Above the montane forest, the subalpine zone is a parkland mix of groves and meadows where the trees are still growing upright. Further up the mountain, trees become shrubby and grow along the ground. This tree form is called "krummholz," the German word for

crooked wood. In the Cascades, the species of trees that grow this way are considered alpine species and define the alpine zone. So the timberline really extends from the montane forest to the alpine zone. Winter snow loads determine the timber line in the Cascades, both because they slow development of soils and they limit the growing season.

A network of trails provides an array of options for exploring the meadow, subalpine and alpine terrain. If you start at Clark Creek Sno-park, you'll cross the bridge at Clark Creek in shady forest of firs and huckleberry. Passing several trail junctions, stay on the Elk Meadows Trail to the meadow. The 1 1/4-mile perimeter trail around the meadow keeps hikers from crisscrossing through fragile habitat. This makes a fine destination for a round trip of almost seven miles.

If you'd like to explore on a longer loop, you can stay on Elk Meadow Trail to the north end of the meadow and a junction with Gnarl Ridge Tie Trail #652A. This takes you to Gnarl Ridge Trail #652 which intersects the Timberline Trail #600 and open meadows of lupine, cat's ears, and jacob's ladder. Make a brief side trip north to the ridgetop for great view of Mt. Hood and Hood River Valley. To return, head south on Timberline Trail to Newton Creek. Cross the creek (carefully!) and watch for the junction with the Newton Creek Trail #646. This will bring you back down to the Elk Meadow Trail and the trailhead, for a total hike of about ten miles.

14
Heather Canyon

The Mountain's Flowered Skirt

Recommended Seasons: August
Use: Light
Difficulty: Moderate

▥ MAPS

Mt. Hood National Forest, Green Trails
Mt. Hood, Oreg #462, Geo-Graphics
Mount Hood Wilderness.

▥ DIRECTIONS

Take U.S. Highway 26 to State Highway
35 north. Exit at Mt. Hood Meadows
and drive to the gate at the end of the
road. Park along the side of the road,
walk around the gate and through the
parking lot, staying right toward utility
buildings on the northeast side. A gravel road goes behind the buildings and
up the hill. Follow it up the hill, watching for an intersection with the
Timberline Trail #600. Head to the right
on the trail and hike about two miles.
When you get to Heather Canyon, you'll
know it.

The meadows of Heather Canyon are
truly voluptuous. Like many other moist
sections of the Timberline Trail, the
sun-drenched meadows of the
mountain's southeast flank put on an
incredible display in summer. Heather
Canyon seems especially dazzling,
perhaps because these wetland
meadows are so lush. Here the glaciated
mountain peak is framed by tumbling
water and expanses of dancing flowers
in rainbow colors.

Yellow and magenta monkey flowers
burst from the tumbled rocks and
mossy crevices. Lupine mirror the

intense blue of an alpine sky on a
summer day. Tangerine-orange Indian
paintbrush sways in breezes that blow
through ravines like breath from the
mountain. In open upland meadows,
Douglas asters bend in lavender ripples.

For the flowers, this is a fast-paced
world. All winter, skiers practice telemark
turns on the steep snows that blanket the
meadows from November through June.
The threat of a freeze lurks even in mid
summer. These meadows have a very
short and therefore intense growing
season. While flowers appear here as soon
as the snow has melted, the entire
mountainside bursts into bloom in early
August. There's nothing casual or
haphazard about this timing. These
flowers want to reproduce and they put
on one heck of an extravaganza to do so.

Most native wildflowers in the
Pacific Northwest are perennials.
Perennials are soft-stemmed plants
that emerge from the ground in spring,
grow and flower and produce seeds,
then die back with the first hard freeze
and remain dormant during the winter.
Perennials may live only a few seasons
or many years but they remain in the
same place, establishing a strong root
system that helps them withstand
changes in temperature and moisture.

There are great advantages to
sinking roots deep into the ground, but
when it comes to reproducing, immobility
has some serious drawbacks. Plants
can't go out and find a mate. They're

A winter ski run freed of snow in August is carpeted in Douglas asters.

stuck in one spot. So they use an intermediary, a surrogate lover who carries, if not love letters, at least the sexy powder that will make more little flowers next year—pollen.

Instead of courting each other, flowers court pollinators. Over time, flowers have found creative ways of enticing reliable couriers to carry the male messages (pollen) to the female seed-making parts of the flowers. The

messengers are none other than humble bumble bees.

There are at least 600 native bees in the Pacific Northwest. Here in the flowery meadows of the mountain on a summer afternoon, it is easy to spot a dozen different species of wild bees buzzing from flower to flower. The color of their pollen sacks, ranging from lemonade yellow to burnt umber, provides clues to their flower travels. Of

temperatures. They can do this because their bodies are covered with an insulating coat of fur and composed primarily of flight muscles which they can vibrate and warm. When a bumble emerges from its burrow on a crisp morning, it jiggles until its little body is warm enough to take flight. It is no wonder that they happily carry pollen from flower to flower in high-elevation meadows like Heather Canyon, Paradise Park and Cairn Basin on Mt. Hood.

these wild bees, the one that is easiest to identify is the fuzzy bumble.

Because they are particularly well adapted to the cold, bumbles have been found in the some of the world's harshest climates including the Arctic Circle where their life cycle may be as short as two weeks. While domesticated honey bees disdain cold wet weather, and won't fly until the sun shines, bumbles fly in rain and very cold

A rainbow of monkey flower, lupine and paintbrush.

Azure seas of lupine perfume the air.

Bumble bees differ from honey bees in other ways. They have a gentle manor and while they're equipped with stingers, they use them only when seriously provoked. They also have tongues much longer than honey bees so they are able to draw nectar from flowers the honey bee couldn't touch.

Wild bees have evolved with their flower hosts over thousands of years and each has adapted to take best advantage of the other. For example, bees see a different range of color than humans do. They see violet, blue, yellow, white and ultra violet, but they don't see red. So they are not attracted to red flowers, but those lovely Douglas asters look mighty appealing. We share with the bee the ability to see the pretty light purple color of the aster, but the bee also sees an ultra-violet pattern on the petals that helps direct it to the center of the flower, much like landing lights on an airport runway.

Lupine have a most amazing adaptation. The lupine flower stalk is made up of several flowers that mature over time from bottom to top. Each flower has a lower lip that must be pushed out of the way to put the nectar within reach. Bees have learned to grasp the upper part of the flower and use their back legs to push the lower lip out of the way. When they do this, they expose a pointed pollen tube that squirts pollen onto their bellies.

If you find this as fascinating as I do, here is what I recommend. When you buy your calendar for the upcoming year, open it to the first week in August and before any other commitment can get in the way, make a date with the mountain. Make sure you are here to see this magnificent dance of life. And remember that without the bees, there would be no flowers. As you exult in the ecstacy of a summer day in a wildflower extravaganza, take time to thank the tiny fuzzy bees who make it all possible.

This hike is on the eastern stretch of the Timberline Trail #600 (Hike #11). Heather Canyon deserves its own listing because it is one of the most spectacular wildflower displays I have ever seen, and the route described here is one of the easiest and shortest connecting routes to the Timberline Trail, thus providing you with a modest day hike as compared to other similar trails.

Tumbling water and swaying wildflowers define Heather Canyon.

15

Parkdale Lava Beds

Black Rocks and Red Apples

Recommended Seasons: Spring, Summer, and Fall
Use: Light
Difficulty: Easy

▦ MAPS

Mount Hood National Forest, Geo-Graphics Mount Hood Wilderness.

▦ DIRECTIONS

From Hood River take State Highway 35 south and follow signs to the community of Parkdale. Drive into town, and turn left (south) at the Mt. Hood Railroad depot onto Clear Creek Road and head toward the mountain following signs to Lawrence Lake. You will curve around a large meadow then enter forest. As you enter national forest land, this becomes Forest Road 2840. Watch for a small reservoir on the left. It empties into an aquaduct that goes under the road. Drive over the aquaduct, then watch for a fairly obscure forest road on the right. It is not the one that follows the aqueduct, but the next one. Turn right onto this road and park at the end. There is no trailhead.

The landscape around Mount Hood was shaped by the massive forces that created the mountain itself and its snow-capped cousins up and down the Cascade Range. Over millions of years, these big cones gushed lava, shot house-sized boulders, and blew ash to the four winds.

While we often think of volcanic eruptions as events that took place when dinosaurs were cruising through, in fact the Pacific Northwest is part of a larger circle of volcanic activity surrounding the Pacific Ocean called the Pacific Rim that is very active today. While perhaps a bit more tranquil than it was a couple million years ago, it has been a mere twenty years since Mt. Hood's cousin to the north blew her top. And just a bit over 100 years since Mt. Lassen in Northern California erupted. The west coast of the United States, Hawaii and Japan are all part of this volatile ring where large plates shift and shove, jiggling us in earthquakes and sending up lava, smoke, and steam.

If you want to see first-hand some of the most resent rock formations around Mt. Hood, you don't need an ice axe and crampons. Instead, pack a picnic, pop the kids in the car and head for Parkdale. One of Mount Hood National Forest's best kept secrets is right here in this charming little community located on the flanks of Mt. Hood.

Parkdale is a small village nestled into the upper Hood River Valley amid apple and pear orchards. From here, you'll enjoy splendid views of both Mt. Hood to the south, and Mt. Adams to the north across the Columbia River in Washington. Parkdale graciously welcomes guests to its gift shops, antique stores, cafes and a microbrewery.

On the outskirts of town, in some cases in the backyards of some townsfolk, rises a massive mound of black crumbly-looking lava. Much of the lava rests within the national forest. If you try to find your way to it, you will probably meet with frustration and do a fair amount of trespassing on private property as I did. But I discovered the secret.

Head out of town south toward Lawrence Lake and you'll find a small road that leads to the big black rock pile. It isn't easy to find, and there is no trail to the lavabeds. Information folks at the Hood River Ranger Station can point to it on the map, but this isn't a recognized recreation site, so you have to poke around a bit and use some intuition to find your way. The Geo-Graphics map shows the road clearly. Wear sturdy boots and bring some gloves, because once you get there you'll want to scramble a bit and the rocks are sharp.

It seems about 7000 years ago, basaltic andesite lava gurgled out of a cinder cone vent here. Lava often bubbles when it reaches the earth's surface, much as a carbonated beverage fizzes when the bottle cap is popped, even though it remains clear when under pressure in the bottle. The lava oozed for three miles toward the Columbia River, covering a two-square-mile area. It redirected the Middle Fork of Hood River. And just to make things exciting, it hurled large basalt boulder "bombs." The mineral-rich soil of the Hood River Valley that today nurtures apple and pear trees, started out as basalt boulders and ash.

While at the Parkdale Lava beds, promise you will not go poking around in the little dark holes in the lava. These lava tubes provide homes for bats. Biologists are just beginning to study their use of the lava beds. What they do know is that they are very delicate little creatures that must remain undisturbed, as slight changes in temperature can stress or even kill them.

Autumn at the lava beds is spectacular. Vine maples' vivid red foliage is a knockout against the backdrop of black lava. Nearby dogwoods and big-leaf maples are dressed in complementary autumn hues and the apples are at their best. After your adventure, head back to Parkdale's orchards and stock up on fresh fruit. You can pick up a brochure at many Parkdale businesses that provides a map and listing of local orchards. My favorite is Mt Hood Organic Farms at the end of

Firey wine maples erupt from the dark basalt.

This pastoral view greets visitors headed to the lava beds.

Smullen Road. There you'll find fresh heirloom varieties of apples and pears grown organically. And the owners John and Brady Jacobson must have the best view of Mt. Hood in the whole upper Hood River Valley.

You prefer spring? Then the flowering dogwoods light up the forest, while in the upper valley, apple orchards toss a fluttering confetti of petals to the wind. Hood River Valley celebrates Blossom Festival in April.

■ OTHER OPTIONS

You could make the Parkdale Lavabeds a first stop on the way to a longer hike. Several trails that begin on roads above Lawrence Lake connect with the north side of the Timberline Trail #600, including Pinnacle Ridge Trail #630 and Elk Cove Trail #631. Call the Hood River Ranger Station for information on these hikes.

Pear and apple orchards produce a sweet autumn harvest.

High Prairie

16

Trail # 493, Divide Trail #468

A Room with a View

Recommended Seasons: Early summer for flowers, fall for raptors
Use: Light
Difficulty: Moderate

MAPS

Mt. Hood National Forest, Columbia Wilderness and Badger Creek Wilderness.

DIRECTIONS

To start your hike at High Prairie, take State Highway 35 to the east side of Mt. Hood and head east on Forest Road 44. In 3.8 miles turn right (south) on High Prairie Road 4410. Just shy of five miles you'll reach a T intersection, turn left and pull into the trailhead parking lot. You can also start from the trailhead at the base of Flag Point Lookout Road. From Forest Road 44, take 4420 south. In about two miles, 4420 heads right, but you head left on 2730. Follow it about a mile past Fifteen Mile Campground and watch for signs to Flag Point Lookout. You'll turn right on rough dirt Forest Road 200 and follow it up the hill for three miles to trailhead parking and an obscure trailhead. A short hike south takes you to the gated road to the lookout.

If you've ever been curious about fire lookouts, here's your chance to see one up close and personal. You can

Rock outcrops on the Divide Trail provide expansive views.

make a very long round trip from High Prairie along the Divide Trail to Flag Point Lookout and back, a total of almost 17 miles. Or you can drive up a rough road to a trailhead close to the lookout and begin your adventure there. Or split the difference with a car shuttle.

From the eastern end of the Divide Trail, if you walk through the gated area and up the road a short distance, you arrive at the base of the Flag Point Lookout tower where you can see the building structure and a great view. Flag Point Lookout is staffed during fire season, the tower serving as the hired lookout's residence and active work site. Therefore, use discretion when visiting and only enter the tower staircase and landing if you are invited to do so.

The Divide Trail connects Flag Point, elevation 5651 feet, with Lookout Mountain, elevation 6525 feet. Lookout Mountain is the second-highest peak in Mt. Hood National Forest and as its name implies was the site of a fire lookout, too. These sites, along with 137 other high-elevation points across this forested landscape, provided vantage points from which to monitor lightning strikes and new fires or "smokes." While the technology of firefighting has greatly advanced in recent years, the Forest Service still staffs a few lookouts full time during the summer and early fall, and staffs others during periods when lightning is forecasted.

The original fire lookouts were just people. They were young men employed by the Forest Service during the summer season who were expected to hike to one or two high points each day and look for smoke. When firefighting graduated to a serious vocation and became a primary mission of the Forest Service, the agency decided to provide appropriate accommodations for the people expected to spend each working day scanning the horizon.

In 1915, the Forest Service developed a standard architecture. The prototype for the "D-6 Cupola" was the lookout station placed on the summit of Mt. Hood. This little 12-by-12-foot house had windows all around with a little upper story used as an observatory. Tested in this most formidable environment, it became the standard, used on mountain tops in Idaho, Montana, Oregon, and Washington.

The Mt. Hood lookout survived 26 winters. It was abandoned in 1935, determined to be too impractical because it so often was enveloped in clouds. Two years later the district ranger climbed up to inspect it and found its pumice foundation had shifted and eroded so badly that a third of the structure was standing on thin air over the north side of the summit. During the winter of 1941, the little structure blew off the mountain top entirely, landing in a crevasse on Eliot Glacier where it still resides today.

A series of lookout designs followed. After the elegant little two-story structures built in the 1920s came the forties look, the familiar shuttered square buildings, some with hipped roofs. By

Flag Point Lookout is staffed during fire season but can be rented from November to May.

76 High Prairie 16

the 1970s, the Forest Service was building plywood lookouts with flat roofs, an improvement in terms of initial cost, with a sad deterioration in charm. Lookout Mountain and Flag Point have each been crowned by a series of buildings with these designs.

As the second-highest point in the forest, Lookout Mountain was an ideal spot from which to scan the terrain. It sported a lookout structure from 1911 until 1960. The first was a log cabin in the meadow below the summit, followed by several cabins on ten-foot platforms. In 1940, these were replaced with the familiar wood-frame precut little house with shutters, mounted on a ten-foot platform. The lookout was maintained until the 1960s.

Flag Point, twelve miles southeast of Mt. Hood, got its first lookout building in 1924. The six-by-six-foot building sat atop a forty-foot pole tower. Flag Point, too, saw a series of buildings, replaced about every decade. The lookout that stands here today is a fourteen-foot square building on a sixty-foot tower of treated timbers, built in the 1960s. Staffed in the summer, it can be rented from November to May as an intriguing and unorthodox winter getaway spot.

The role of the fire lookout has always had a bit of romance attached to it. In fact, many a honeymoon has been spent in these little buildings. The job actually has some demands. Lookouts take regular scans of the horizon and readings from nearby weather equipment. When a smoke is spotted, they are expected to call the local ranger station and as accurately as possible, report the fire's location using an Osborne Firefinder. The instrument swivels over a circular map on a stand in the center

Scarlet Indian paintbrush punctuates the rocky terrain.

of the lookout building. Similar to a surveyor's transit, it allows the user to relate a distant smoke column to other features of the landscape in order to precisely pinpoint its location.

About the time that Lookout Mountain was getting its first log cabin, William B. Osborne was hard at work in his engineering office developing this fire-finding instrument. Other models have been developed over the years, but the one still used today is Osborne's 1934 model.

The Forest Service still hires people to staff its lookouts. Many are school teachers, students or writers who can pull away from other obligations to work

Photo by Tom Iraci.

six days a week in a remote location in July, August and September. Flag Point is a choice post, as it is within a reasonable commute to Hood River.

Between Flag Point and Lookout Mountain is perhaps the finest trail in Badger Creek Wilderness. The Divide trail follows the top of a high rugged ridge of craggy rocks dotted with exquisite little natural rock gardens. Penstemon, lupine, paintbrush and alpine antennaria emerge from the boulders. Sedums stay low, tucking themselves between the rocks to bronze in the summer sun. In mid summer, enough snow remains for a seat-of-the-pants slide down a frosty embankment.

Most of the trail follows the crest, but the middle stretch briefly descends through forest along the back side of the ridge to avoid some of the most precipitous terrain. Here you'll come to a junction with the Fret Creek Trail to Oval Lake, a tiny shallow puddle.

From the crest, the views are expansive. To the south, Badger Lake gleams. In September migrating raptors glide by on warm air currents (see Hike #19) and in October the larch trees turn golden, like yellow birthday candles scattered through the forest.

For informatio n on renting Flag Point, Five Mile or Clear Lake lookouts, call Barlow Ranger Station.

School Canyon

Trail #468
Little Badger Creek Trail #469

Schooling in Native Plants

Recommended Seasons: Spring, summer

Use: Light

Difficulty: School Canyon is moderate, Little Badger is strenuousf

■ MAPS

Mt. Hood National Forest, Columbia Wilderness and Badger Creek Wilderness, *Oregon Atlas & Gazetteer* (DeLorme).

■ DIRECTIONS

From I-84 in the Columbia River Gorge, take Exit 87 and head south on U.S. Highway 197. Drive through the charming town of Dufur (Barlow Ranger Station is located here), continue south 3 miles and watch for signs directing you to the community of Friend. You'll veer right onto Dufur Gap Road. In about six miles at Hix Road, take a right and in about a third of a mile take a left. You are now on Friend Road which will take you to Friend. Stop at the old school on the left, then continue west into the national forest. When the road forks, head south on Forest Road 27. Watch for School Canyon Trailhead on the right. Little Badger Creek Trailhead is three miles beyond.

From the west, take Highway 26 to Highway 35

north. Take Forest Road 44 east, turn right on 4420. In two miles take the fork to the left. This becomes 2730 and after several miles joins Forest Road 27. Follow 27 south about 8 miles. School Canyon Trailhead is on the right. Continue three miles to Little Badger Trailhead.

Who knows why this place is called School Canyon? Perhaps there was a school here years ago. It is one of the finest trails I've seen for exploring our least-known forest plant community, the pine oak woodland. But before you arrive at the pines and oaks, take a drive through the rolling, rocky grasslands east of the forest and south of Dufur. This route will take you through one of my favorite Oregon landscapes, to a classic one-room schoolhouse, circa

Lupine, balsam root and paintbrush bloom in crayon colors.

Photo by Robin Dobson

Balsam root bursts into sunny bloom beneath a spring moon.

1909, in the little "community" of Friend. There is really nothing there but the schoolhouse, but it's worth a stop, for it is a gem.

I'm a sucker for old schools. They smell and feel like a thousand September mornings, full of new shoes and pencils and butterflies in the stomach. I went to school in one and even lived in one for 15 years. They are a vanishing legacy and worth treasuring. This one still welcomes octogenarian alumni each June for a reunion. The Friend School functions as a community center and the door has been unlocked each time I've visited. Stop by and glimpse a sweet bit of Oregon's past.

Now you're ready for the hike. Combining Little Badger Creek Trail and School Canyon Trail, you will ven-

ture through the greatest variety of plant communities I have seen in Mt. Hood National Forest. The Badger Creek Wilderness is where east meets west. Moist Cascades conifer forests meet the arid treeless Columbia Plateau. There isn't a dividing line, but rather an intriguing intermingling of both ecosystems. Within this zone, a unique forest and grassland species mix—the pine oak woodland—extends from the northern boundary of the Warm Springs Reservation to the Columbia River Gorge. It is a parklike mix of tall stately evergreens and gnarled, dwarfed Oregon white oaks.

The dry east side of Mt. Hood is more hospitable to early season hikes than wet western slopes where heavy snow

The pine oak woodland comes alive in spring.

packs last well into the summer. The wildflower displays here are exquisite and arrive early, when months of gray skies have left westsiders aching for a chance to indulge in unfettered spring giddiness. The show starts in April and peaks in May. It's best to call the Barlow Ranger Station to check road and trail conditions. Often you can get a wildflower report, too.

I recommend you leave a bike at the School Canyon Trailhead and start your hike on the Little Badger Creek Trail because it gets very steep just before you reach the junction and I prefer to save my knees by going up steep sections rather than down. In addition, you'll go up a breezy shady creek versus along the dry ridge. The Little Badger Creek Trail at first climbs gradually, never far from the creek, through moist forest. In the western Cascades, the vegetation along streams, the "riparian area," is similar to that in the adjacent forest. But Mt. Hood blocks rain clouds and greedily keeps their moisture on its western flanks. Badger Creek Wilderness stays high and dry. Here

there is a sharper distinction between the moisture-loving riparian vegetation and the drought-tolerant upland species. Along the creek you'll find cottonwood, alder, western redcedar, big leaf maple, cow parsnip and vine maple plus dozens of tender wild flowers. Calypso bulbosa or fairy slipper, a delicate pink orchid that is extremely fussy about its habitat, pops its spunky head up here and there. Fawn lilies dance across the valley floor.

After three miles and six stream crossings, you'll come to what's left of a miner's cabin. The roof is gone and the walls are crumbling. It seems Tom Kinzel was a prospector, miner, and Forest Service employee who apparently didn't strike it rich on whatever he was digging. Here the trail leaves the valley floor, passes Kinzel Mine, and heads up for a 1000-foot elevation gain in the next half mile. Take your time, the views are great.

High on the ridge, juniper crouch and cling to parched soil and weathered rock, each shielding itself with a coat of chartreuse wolf lichen. Western juniper grows in sites too dry even for ponderosa pines. Watch for Mariposa and fawn lilies as you cross this exposed rocky top in spring.

At four miles you come to the junction with School Canyon Trail #468. Here you begin a gradual descent under lichen-covered hanging rock walls and giant pines. Oddly enough, Pacific dogwood trees are scattered throughout this forest, displaying dazzling white blooms in spring and gumdrop-colored leaves in fall. The trail angles along the

Remains of Tom Kinzel's cabin.

north side of Ball Point where a midsummer bloom of Washington lilies is likely to knock your socks off in a cloud of rich perfume. Rare and usually solitary, these white beauties with pink blush grow here clustered in dozens.

Finally, this trail enters a surreal forest of gnarled stunted oaks. These are not the stately oaks with spreading limbs and elegant architecture so often found in fields in Oregon City or throughout the Willamette Valley. These trees have lived hard and they show it. Yet oak seedlings can be seen sprouting everywhere, seeming to regenerate happily here. In late spring, this oak pine woodland erupts in riotous color, carpeted by Indian paintbrush, lupine, and sunflower-like balsam root. Eastern Oregon ranch and farm lands spread out before you and to the south catch views of Mt. Jefferson and the Three Sisters. As an added bonus, I saw no poison oak anywhere on this trail, which is a treat, as it tends to be the ever-present nasty little buddy of oak trees.

Friend School provides a charming step back in time.

18
Crane Prairie, Boulder Lake

Trail # 478 and Trail # 464
Wet Meadow Habitat

Recommended Seasons: Summer, Fall
Use: Light
Difficulty: Moderate

MAPS

Mount Hood National Forest, Columbia Wilderness and Badger Creek Wilderness, Green Trails Mount Hood OR #462.

DIRECTIONS

From Highway 35, turn south on Forest Road 48 at White River SnoPark. Follow this wide paved road approximately seven miles to Forest Road 4890. Travel southeast through young forest. You'll come to a junction for Road 4891 to Bonney Meadow. This takes you directly to Bonney Meadow Campground, but if you value your tires and suspension system, at the junction take 4881 instead. You can head to Little Boulder Lake by taking 4890-122 then 4890-123. Another option, continue on 4881 to 4880. This will lead you to the Crane Creek Trailhead #463. Use your maps. There are a number of roads and trails through here and you need to keep your bearings.

This beautiful little spot just outside the Badger Creek Wilderness, is largely undiscovered. Within this general area you can find several delightful adventures, depending on whether you want a relaxed stroll along a lake shore or a

Badger Lake from Windy Saddle.

strenuous hike through a lush garden of meadow wildflowers.

Because I prefer circular routes, I seek loop trails whenever possible. To appease my desire for circles and the esoteric sense of closure they give me, I happened to turn my visit to Crane Prairie into a very long hike partly on roads and partly on some of the worst trail I've ever been on. It reinforced that sage advice, "call the information center for road and trail information before heading out." So listen up. You can have a delightful adventure by learning from my mistake.

From the road next to Little Boulder Lake, pop into the woods and you'll find the pretty little lake framed by a rock cliff. Head north on the Boulder Lake Trail. You'll come to a junction for Spinning Lake and Crane Creek. Head east on this trail. It will cross Road 4881 [an alternative route] and head through beautiful moist forest and across the bridge over Boulder Creek. Above you the talus slope is dotted with aspen. These lovely trees are called quaking or trembling aspen for the motion of their leaves in the wind, a golden shimmer in an October breeze.

The trail is called Crane Creek Trail #464 but it follows Boulder Creek. In 1924, in an effort to reduce the number of duplicate geographic names, the Forest Service changed the name to Crane Creek, to harmonize with Crane Prairie. In 1977, through the efforts of a group of citizens, it was changed back to Boulder Creek.

The trail parallels the creek for the first couple of miles through small flowery meadows alternating with shady dells. Bunchberry dogwood clusters between the roots of big firs and columbine's dangling orange lanterns line the trail. Dozens of tiny green frogs ask that you kindly step carefully through puddles in the trail.

In a couple of miles you'll enter Crane Prairie. Here Crane Prairie Trail heads to the left, while Crane Creek Trail heads right. The wet prairie is lush with wildflowers that emerge just as snows melt and continue in wave after wave through the summer. In May, marsh marigold and buttercup color the wet areas. In June, steer's head, that relative of bleeding heart with a single pink and white flower shaped like a horned cow's head, enjoys the early-season moisture. Skunk cabbage appears to float in small pools, its golden-yellow blooms top giant exotic leaves that look like dinosaur food. In the northeast corner of the prairie in mid June six different violets can be found blooming simultaneously.

Following Crane Creek Trail to the right takes you straight up the hill. This section is a grunt but eventually brings you to Windy Saddle, a ridge line above Badger Lake. Road 4860 runs the length of the saddle and the trailhead for the lake begins directly across the road. If you've just grunted up that hill through a warm humid prairie you owe yourself a dip in Badger Lake. Look down there. How can you resist? The Badger Lake Trail #479 is a bit steep but it is only a mile.

Windy campground is flowery and relatively bug-free, even in July.

86 Crane Prairie, Boulder Lake

I happened on this just as the trail crews were cleaning it up. If there is a heaven, the people who clear trails must be assured a place there. They brave the steamiest, buggy conditions on steep slopes hacking at thorny stems and shoveling stoney soil to make our little hikes more pleasant. Bless their hearts.

Make the mile descent and dip your toes, or more of you, into the lake. You probably won't be alone as this is one of the more popular spots in this neck of the woods. Amazingly enough, people haul trailers and motor homes on another one of those really bad forest

roads to camp in comfort at Badger Lake. Expect company.

Back on Windy Saddle, head west. In a half mile, you'll come to Camp Windy Campground. I'm sure this place might throw you a gale in the right conditions, but on a clear summer afternoon it is one of the prettiest camping spots I've seen. The breeze is a help here in late June and early July to keep bugs at bay.

You can make a full loop out of this if you choose to bushwhack to Trail 689 (again, use your map) and follow it down to the junction with Crane Prairie Trail #464. But here's the rub, Crane

This rustic bridge makes an easy crossing over Boulder Creek.

Prairie Trail is really wet in the early part of the summer and when I was last there it hadn't been maintained. I arrived there late in the day, the signs were down, there were a lot of blown-down trees and the mud was deep. I was very relieved to make it back to Crane Creek Trail.

This makes for a long 14-plus-mile loop. Again, check the status of the trail with the local Forest Service office. If it is later in the summer and the trail has dried out a bit, Crane Prairie Trail will provide a beautiful forest hike, joining Crane Creek Trail in the prairie.

Otherwise, from Camp Windy, you can backtrack on the road and hop back on Crane Creek Trail retracing your steps.

I learned about this spot from a Forest Service backcountry ranger who came here from New Jersey. This is one of his favorite places and I'm sure he hoped it wouldn't appear here, remaining his little secret. Sorry Jim, here it is. What he told me was right, it is special.

Photo by Tom Iraci.

Skunk cabbage is a jaunty perch for this roughskin newt.

Butterflies, moths and bees dance through the prairie.

Bonney Butte

Soaring Raptors

Corner photo by Dan Sherman.

Recommended Seasons: Fall
Use: Light
Difficulty: Moderate

MAPS

Mount Hood National Forest, Columbia Wilderness and Badger Creek Wilderness, Geo-Graphics Mount Hood Wilderness, Green Trails Mt. Hood OR No. 462.

DIRECTIONS

From State Highway 35, turn south on Forest Road 48 at White River Sno-Park. Follow this wide paved road approximately seven miles to Forest Road 4890. Turn left and travel southeast through young forest. You'll come to a junction for Road 4891 to Bonney Meadow. This road is deeply eroded and has sharp rocks. It is best suited to a high-clearance vehicle with good tires.

In September and October if you stand on one of the high ridges on the east side of Mt. Hood, you're liable to feel something very large whoosh past your ear. Before you can gather yourself enough to say "Wow! What was that?" a big-winged carnivore will have left you in the dust and be almost out of view.

You may not think of eagles, hawks and falcons as migratory birds, but each autumn, birds of prey follow predictable annual migration routes around the mountains of the west. One of these routes goes right around the east side of Mt. Hood.

There are three main flyways in the western United States. The Pacific Flyway runs from Canada, through western Washington, Oregon and California. The Intermountain Flyway runs through the Great Basin, and the Rocky Mountain Flyway borders that range. The birds use these routes because they avoid crossing mountains, but also to take advantage of the air flow near the mountain. Warm valley air hits the mountains and flows upward. These warm updrafts or "thermals" take some of the work out of flying, allowing the birds to stop flapping their wings, soar for long distances, and conserve energy.

Hawkwatch International is a non-profit organization founded in 1986 and based in Salt Lake City, Utah. The organization was formed to protect hawks, eagles and other birds of prey through research, education, and conservation. Today, Hawkwatch International counts migrating raptors at fifteen sites in nine states.

Hawkwatch International biologists discovered this flyway around Mt. Hood in the early 1990s and began searching for the best vantage point from which to observe the birds on their annual migration. A good spot for raptor watching is usually high up so that you can get close to the flying birds. It also is a spot where the terrain concentrates the birds over that high land form. Hawkwatch biologists picked Bonney Butte. Since 1994, biologists and volunteers have camped on the butte during migration season from early September to early November, counting, capturing, and banding the birds in order to learn more about them.

They use two types of nets to capture the flying raptors. One called a mist net, is very fine netting held upright by three poles. The other, called a bow net, springs up and closes like a clam shell. Each of these is baited with a very frightened looking starling or English sparrow, held on a string by a tiny leather vest. The vest protects the bait bird's body while allowing its wings to flap to attract the flying raptor.

When a raptor zeros in on the bait bird as prey, it flies into the net. Volunteers dash out of hiding and capture the raptor, contain it and place a metal band on its leg, then release it. The band identifies where and when it was captured. Should this bird be captured again at this site or one of the other banding stations throughout the west, researchers will collect data from the band in hopes of understanding the birds' migration behavior and patterns. (Bait birds, by the way, get every other day off and if injured, they are retired from service and receive a tiny purple heart.)

Breezy days are best for banding, when the raptors are sailing through on the winds. On windless days, raptors fly low taking them out of range for capture on the butte. Volunteers can still see them to count them. This banding station counts more merlins than any other site in the country. Volunteers compile an average count of 1500-2500 raptors each season and on average band 100 of the birds.

You can watch raptors riding thermals from high ridges east of Mt. Hood including High Prairie and the Divide Trail (Hike #16). Or you can head up to the top of Bonney Butte where volunteers will be glad to show you what they are doing, and even recruit you to help watch for incoming birds. The one-mile road to the top of the butte is kept gated, but you can hike past the gate. A sign on the road directs visitors to the banding station at the top. Bring warm clothes and binoculars.

For more information on HawkWatch International, visit their website.

Entry sign provides raptor information.

Photo by Dan Sherman.

Volunteer displays wing markings of prairie falcon.

Photo by Dan Sherman.

Bonney Meadow

Trail #471, Kane Springs
Trail #463, Boulder Lake Trail #473
Healing Plants

Recommended Seasons: Spring, Summer, Fall
Use: Light
Difficulty: Easy from campground, Moderate from Boulder Lake

■ MAPS

Mount Hood National Forest, Columbia Wilderness and Badger Creek Wilderness Geo-Graphics Mount Hood Wilderness, Green Trails Mt. Hood OR No 462.

■ DIRECTIONS

From State Highway 35, turn south on Forest Road 48 at White River Sno-Park. Follow this wide paved road approximately seven miles to Forest Road 4890. Turn left and travel southeast through young forest. You'll come to a junction for Road 4891 to Bonney Meadow. This takes you directly to Bonney Meadow Campground, but if you value your tires and suspension system, continue 1/2 mile and turn onto 4890-122 to 4890-123. This places you at a dead end right next to Little Boulder Lake.

I visited Bonney Meadow on a Tuesday in early July. I looked forward to some solitary car camping, some reading, and a bit of hiking near this petite flowery meadow. I had been warned that the road was in poor condition. Although I had worried that my car would lack clearance to make the trek

through deep ruts, it turns out that the real problem with the road is its frighteningly jagged rocks. I expected at any moment to hear a loud popping sound followed by a hiss. I was quite relieved when I finally spotted the sign directing me to the right into Bonney Meadow Campground.

There to my surprise were five cars and a dozen women with several small children. I snarled. Time to mentally shift gears. I wasn't going to get much solitude. But I wasn't about to turn right around and drive back over that road.

Sometimes life is so good at pulling the rug out from under you, just when you feel you've determined your path. Sometimes those rug-pullings turn out to be serendipity. In this case I happened to have popped in on a yearly reunion of women who study medicinal plants. They gather at the meadow, relax in each other's company with their children, and botanize to their heart's content. Some years nearly fifty people come and go over the course of a week.

While I'd normally be concerned at so many people gathering near a delicate meadow, I felt reassured that these women treasured the native plants that grow here and would take care not to trample or disturb the meadow's living creatures. And I felt I had a brief view into an ancient experience, for women

Yellow monkey flower blooms near a rustic bridge.

have been coming together to gather medicinal plants in the forest since time immemorial.

When native people of the Columbia River Gorge, or bands of the Clackamas or Molalla people were injured or became ill, they went to the medicine cabinet, much as we do today. Their "medicine cabinet" probably looked more like a leather pouch. From it they would choose an appropriate salve, poultice, tea or tonic to relieve pain and purge toxins. Usually the women were the keepers of the community's knowledge of the healing properties of plants and other natural materials.

Each summer, as they collected the varied plants that rounded out their diets, they also restocked the medicine cabinet. Centuries of accumulated experience made these healers expert in choosing specific parts of certain plants at the time of the season when their healing properties were strongest. These plants were then carefully preserved, usually through drying, to retain their freshness and value as medicine.

Over a season, dozens of plants grow and flower in this lovely little meadow. The trail around Bonney Meadow is an easy stroll with views across the meadow to Mt. Hood. If you do camp here, dine early, then stroll a bit north of the meadow for a pastel evening alpenglow display on Mt. Hood. Having said good night to the mountain, stroll back to your camp and listen to the night creatures that love this moist meadow environment.

If you choose to avoid the crazy road into Bonney Meadow, you can follow the directions for Crane Prairie (Hike #18) and hike to the meadow from Boulder Lake. From the lake, backtrack along the road and watch for the Trail #463

You'll have Boulder Lake to yourself on weekdays in July.

crossing. From this point, the route is gradual up through an old clearcut. The advantage of old clearcuts is that they provide great wildflower habitat for several years until the forest gradually shades out the sun-loving species. Here, you'll hike through firs before reaching the clearcut openings (remember, we are outside the wilderness) for showy early-summer displays of rhodies and bear grass.

The trail skirts a cliff above Boulder Lake before arriving at Bonney Meadow. The meadow provides a rich display of wildflowers and a cool resting spot. Continue past the meadow and descend through boulder fields that would make any pika happy. This makes a delightful loop and places you back at a great location to start your next adventure.

You can also take Bonney Meadow Trail #471 which starts from the 4891

tle hay makers, they carry big mouthfuls of grass to their burrows until they have accumulated a bale or two by season's end. Tucked into dry spots between boulders, the hay provides enough food for the pika all winter that it doesn't need to hibernate. Seemingly easy prey for lithe predators like weasels, pikas often ditch their predator by using the familiar pile like a maze. They also set up such a ruckus that other pikas join the chase, running around frantically and confusing the poor weasel.

Mountain heliotrope is a disinfectant and perfume.

Road near Bonney Meadow and runs down to White River and the Catalpa Lake Trail. Bonney Meadow Trail is extemely steep near the trailhead on Forest Road 4891. It levels out at the bottom, but can be a bit tricky to follow.

PIKAS

If you hear a high-pitched "eenk" from the rock piles above Boulder Lake, you've been sternly warned by the mighty pika to steer clear of its personal talus slope. Despite their attempts at intimidation, pikas are pretty small to be making such a big sound. They look similar to bunnies but with guinea pig ears. In fact, both rabbits and pikas are in the Lagomorpha order, a grouping of critters formerly lumped in with rodents.

Pikas are found in rock piles throughout the Cascades. Known as lit-

Pikas squeak at intruders.

CLACKAMAS RIVER NORTH
Oak Grove Fork, Roaring River

21

Memaloose Lake

Trail #515
Forest Succession and Plant Communities

Recommended Seasons: Spring, Summer, Fall
Use: Heavy
Difficulty: Strenuous

MAPS
Mount Hood National Forest, Green Trails Map #492 Fish Creek Mtn.

DIRECTIONS
From Estacada, take Highway 224 south for 9 1/3 miles and turn right in Forest Road 45, crossing the Memaloose Bridge. The road is steep and is a single lane with double lanes on the corners. Follow the road 12 miles, past the junction of Road 4550. The trailhead is well marked on the left, and parking is on the right.

Inside out flower and merten's coral root.

Pick a weekday for this trail. It is the first trail you come to as you enter the Clackamas River Recreation Area from Estacada and this easy access makes it a very popular spot. It isn't an easy trail. With an elevation gain of 1200 feet in a mile and a half, it makes you breathe hard. For that reason, this trail deserves a leisurely pace.

The Douglas fir, hemlock and cedar forest is a classic "climax" forest. Forests go through constant change. As the forest matures, one group of plants takes over or "succeeds" the one before. This is known as forest "succession" and the last stage of succession is climax. On the west side of the Cascade Range, when a site is newly opened by a windstorm or fire, the first plants to grow are herbaceous plants like fireweed, and shrubs like ceanothus. Deciduous trees like vine maple and alder may sprout along with sun-loving Douglas firs. When the firs get tall enough to shade the ground, hemlock seedlings take hold. As the forest matures over several hundred years, the hemlock trees shade the ground, preventing young Douglas firs from sprouting and the hemlocks dominate the site. This is called the climax stage of a Douglas fir and hemlock forest.

This description is a gross simplification, as there are a wide number of other plants and a variety of conditions that determine how this process progresses. But by looking at the kinds of trees and their age, you can tell a num-

Oregon ash and alder grow along the moist shore.

ber of things about a forest. Here, the forest has aged to classic old growth. Fire hasn't touched this site for several hundred years. Under the giant firs, cedars, and hemlocks there are 400-year-old yew trees.

The first section of the trail is very moist, with Memaloose Creek and dozens of small springs saturating the soils. The forest floor isn't even visible in places, but instead is a lumpy carpet of thick moss over ancient logs. Decaying nurse logs provide nutrients for a row of young hemlocks, the next generation.

Part of the appeal of this place is the rich array of interesting plants that grow in the damp humus within 1/2 mile of the trailhead. Tucked into this jumble of old trees and downed logs are delightful little wildflowers and interesting bog plants. Much of the forest floor is covered with shamrock-shaped leaves of oxalis. Chewed, they taste like tart green apples and provide a bit of thirst relief on a hot hike. Nearby, bunchberry dog-

wood spreads across the forest floor. In early summer, this elegant ground cover pops up perfect white dogwood blossoms nearly identical to those on a full-sized dogwood tree. The blooms turn to red berries in the late summer and foliage sometimes turns red in the fall.

Among the dogwoods, the slender rosy stem of Merten's coralroot entices both orchid lovers and its small pollinator moth. Coralroot orchids have no leaves nor chlorophyl, so they cannot make their own food as green plants do. Instead, they must get their nutrients from the decaying plants in the soil. To do this, they have worked out a pact with their tiny soil fungus buddies. The roots of these orchids are knobby and small, but the fungus attaches to them then spreads out through the soil, bringing in nutrients from decomposing material for some distance around the plant.

The trail courses through a maze of immense root wads. Vanilla leaf, foam-flower, duckfoot, wild ginger and false

Service berry and beargrass bloom in June.

solomonseal grow up, over and around these exposed roots of fallen giants. Here in perennially wet conditions, the trees don't need to sink deep roots to find moisture. Shallow root systems make them vulnerable to wind storms.

Within a half mile, you leave this very moist forest floor and climb toward Memaloose Lake. Despite the fact that the forest floor and the ridge receive the same amount of rain, the rocky ridge soils drain easily. Drying out earlier in the season, the plant communities that grow here are adapted to drought conditions. The hairy tufts of beargrass soften the scene under delicate small rhododendron and Oregon grape. Drifts of white and pale lavender iris mingle with lupine.

Memaloose Creek tumbles from the lake as you reach its reedy shore. A few campsites are scattered through the forested flat. Memaloose Lake is small, and only five feet deep, making it more appealing for fishing than swimming. It

is stocked regularly with brook trout.

Climb the remaining half mile up and out of Memaloose Lake and you reach the South Fork Mountain Lookout, an abandoned fire lookout site. The 1930s-era lookout structure, a 50-foot tower with an open platform on top, was torn down in the 1960s. Like most lookout sites, the views from here are fantastic.

■ A WORD OF CAUTION

This lake and some of the other recreational sites along the Clackamas River corridor attract a rowdy crowd on weekend evenings. You passed a couple of quarries on the road in. These are always popular shooting areas, often with damage to trees that had the misfortune of growing nearby. The small wilderness toilet graciously provided at Memaloose Lake was full of bullet holes. I hope they weren't put there while it was in use. At any rate, be cautious, particularly when hiking alone.

Emergent wetland surrounds the shallow lake.

Great views can be seen from South Fork Mountain.

Clackamas River

Trail #715
A Wild and Scenic River

Recommended Seasons: Year round
Use: Medium

MAPS

Mt. Hood National Forest, Green Trails Map Fish Creek Mountain #492.

DIRECTIONS

From Estacada, travel 16 miles south on Highway 224 to Forest Road 54. Turn right onto 54. Fish Creek trailhead is on your right across the bridge. Clackamas River Trail begins across from the trailhead parking, just past the end of the bridge. The trail ends at Indian Henry Campground in 7.8 miles.

They say the Clackamas River begins 6000 feet above sea level on the slopes of Olallie Butte. But you really don't see much action there. In reality, the river gushes from a pile of rocks a couple of miles to the northwest. From there it flows nearly 83 miles, swollen by creeks and rivers along its route and draining 940 square miles.

Densely-forested mountainsides, deep rock gorges, hushed old-growth groves, and flowery wet meadows compose the upper watershed. As the river passes the town of Estacada it enters a pastoral landscape. Third-generation farmers and first-generation hobby farmers tap the rich soils of this wandering river's ancestral flood plain. Within the middle watershed, rich river bottom lands sprout Christmas tree plantations; lettuce farms; cows, goats and llamas; black plastic pots of arborvitae; and rows of trellised raspberries.

By the time it flows beneath the Carver Bridge, its banks sport mobile-home parks, warehouses, and suburban tract homes. Five miles from its mouth, it is tapped for tap water. Oregon City, West Linn and Lake Oswego—over 175,000 people—draw 66 million gallons a day from the Clackamas River. Finally, near the city of Gladstone, the waters of the Clackamas blend with the waters of the Willamette and flow to the Columbia and on to the Pacific.

Portland General Electric taps the river's force to turn its turbines and generate electricity from three hydroelectric dams, all equipped with fish ladders. In addition, PGE has two dams on the Oak Grove Fork—one at Timothy Lake and one at Harriet Lake. These are used to hold and slowly release water to the power-generating dams below as well as provide summer recreation. Neither is equipped with fish ladders because they are upstream from natural fish barriers—tall waterfalls. There are a few smaller dams on the river's tributaries.

Nearly 3/4 of the watershed is owned by the public. The upper half lies within Mt. Hood National Forest. Some additional land in the lower watershed is managed by the B.L.M. Clackamas County manages Barton, Eagle Fern, and Metzler

The wild and scenic Clackamas River tumbles through basalt bedrock.

The author feels tiny next to these riverside giants.

Rapids and scenery appeal to kayakers and rafters.

parks, and the state of Oregon manages McIver Park. The highest eastern sections of the Olallie area and the Oak Grove Fork belong to the Confederated Tribes of Warm Springs. The rest is owned privately.

A river the size of the Clackamas, draining such an undulating landscape, is really more a network of rivers than a single body of water. Its headwaters are called the Upper Clackamas, and its mouth the Lower Clackamas. In between, its Oak Grove, North, Middle and South forks converge. It is fed by the Collawash including its Hot Springs Fork, and by Roaring River, Fish Creek, Eagle Creek, Goose Creek, Deep Creek, Richardson Creek, Clear Creek, and

Rock Creek. Dozens of smaller creeks branch off of its upper reaches. Water is the linking element across landscapes, and the Clackamas waters connect a vast and diverse part of both wild and tame Oregon.

The entire upper part of the Clackamas from Olallie Lake Scenic Area to Big Cliff just above the North Fork Reservoir is classed as "Scenic and Recreational" under the Wild and Scenic Rivers Act. More than fourteen miles of the Roaring River is also designated as wild and scenic.

Probably most of us know the Clackamas for the fun we have hiking, driving or fishing along its shores, or floating its waters. How many genera-

Bunchberry dogwood scampers up a fir-tree trunk.

tions of Northwesterners have shared that peculiar ritual of rising in the bleak predawn hours of an autumn Saturday, gulping black coffee as cold drizzle splatters the windshield, only to stand hip-deep in leaden water under dripping skies, hoping to snag a big fish at the end of a skinny line? The thought of it makes me shiver.

Kayakers wriggle into skinny little boats and float like bubbles down the wicked Class III and IV rapids of the upper river. If you would rather watch them than join them, you can often catch sight of colorful little rubberized torpedoes practicing whitewater gymnastics at Bob's Hole.

The Clackamas River Trail is a per-

fect hike for experiencing the features of the river that earned it a designation as wild and scenic. Like the Riverside Trail (Hike #27) it connects two campgrounds along one side of the river. But the experience here is different. The Clackamas River Trail takes you 600 to 800 feet above the river along its canyon walls for glimpses of silvery water through the trees. It crosses rock outcrops, dips into moist stone grottos and dwarfs you beneath giant cedars. Near the halfway point, cross Pup Creek, then take a short side trail to 100 foot Pup Creek Falls. This hike works well as a car or bike shuttle, or you can make a seven-plus-mile round trip hiking to Pup Creek and back from either trailhead.

23

Alder Flat

Trail #574

An Ancient Grove

Corner photo by Tom Iraci

Recommended Seasons: Year round
Use: Medium
Difficulty: Easy

MAPS

Mount Hood National Forest, Green Trails Fish Creek Mtn #492.

DIRECTIONS

Take Highway 224 through Estacada, then southeast for 25 miles. Alder Flat is on the right just northwest of Ripplebrook. Turn right into the well-marked parking lot.

As your hiking boot meets the duff of the Alder Flat Trail, you'll step into a hushed green world of craggy trunks and rubbery lichens. The moss carpet that softens the forest floor is punctuated by sword ferns. A momentary sun ray casts a spotlight on the squishy bark of a reclining log, blown to the ground by some forgotten storm. Along its spine, beads of dew twinkle on the shamrock-shaped leaves of oxalis. The tranquil scene is softened in filtered light, reflected by a million skinny one-inch green shades. Sound is noticeably dampened, too. You have entered a different world.

The ancient forests of the Pacific Northwest possess an aura. It is perhaps this quality of otherworldliness that has captured the imagination, hearts, and political voice of those who have tried to protect them. Often compared to cathedrals, they evoke a sense of the majestic and eternal that some may describe as holy. It is hard not to be awestruck, even if you abstain from spiritual metaphors. In fact, whether explored from the perspective of science or religion, these forests will leave you a changed person. The more you know about them, the more you will be amazed.

Old growth is not merely a forest of old trees. In our rain-drenched temperate river valleys, giant fir trees lurch to the skies like Jack's proverbial bean stalk, gaining 200 feet in height and three feet in girth in less than 100 years. Their counterparts on rocky hillsides with nutrient-poor soil may gain less than a foot in diameter in a century of growth. Old growth really describes the forest structure. Alder Flat is a fine place to wander in the presence of a classic Douglas fir and western hemlock old-growth forest of the western Cascades.

Enter the grove and you will marvel at the big old trees. Douglas fir is the dominant species in westside forests and they grow to immense proportions. Sun-lovers, they reach for the rays, shading the forest floor and any young upstarts that attempt to take their place. Their gnarly branches and dense needles reach across openings to form a lofty forest canopy. As these forests age, elderly hemlocks assert themselves, outlasting the giant Doug firs. On moist riverbanks or lake shores, western redcedars develop massive trunks.

At the shoulders of the giants, vine maples and young hemlocks grow in the shade, providing a middle layer to the forest. On the forest floor, huckleberry, rhododendron, salal, ferns, and dozens of delicate perennials create the lowest layer. This layering of the forest canopy is a key feature of old growth.

Trees that have toppled are known to ecologists as "downed woody debris" and are an important part of the structure of these forests. Punky old giants have as long a life on the ground as they did standing up, taking centuries to gently decompose back into the forest duff. During this process, they hold enormous amounts of water, helping to retain moisture during the Pacific Northwest summer drought. They recycle nutrients

Photo by Tom Iraci.

Spring arrives in the forest when trillium rises from the duff.

Not all of the trees are upright and not all are alive. Standing dead trees are prevalent in these old forests. When you look across a forested valley from a high vantage point, the bleached snags poking up between broken tops of the giant firs are telltale signs that you are looking at an ancient grove. Snags are usually perforated and pock marked by birds that nest in tree-trunk cavities. Pileated woodpeckers are perhaps the best known of these, and their rectangular excavations are easy to identify.

back into soils otherwise quickly depleted through heavy winter rains. A new generation of trees may sprout along the decomposing body of a former giant, called "nurse logs." The gradual demise of these ancient trees provides habitat for the small animals, insects and microorganisms that populate and sustain these forest systems.

There are thousands of other creatures living here, although they are much less noticeable. In fact, the giant trees are completely dependent on the tiniest inhabitants of the forest—the fungi that dwell by the billions in the forest soil. Pick up a slab of fallen bark and peak underneath. The web of white filaments woven through the soil is mycorrhizal fungus. Were it not for these minute forest residents, there would be no big trees. In a complex exchange of services, the tree roots send sugars into the soil to temp the mycorrhizal fungi. In return for the tasty sugars, the fungi wrap around the tree's root tips and process soil nutrients, making them available to the tree.

We usually only see their fruit, the occasional mushroom that emerges from the moss. Fungi that send mushrooms into the light and air, are able to spread spores on the wind. Many fungi remain under the soil, producing truffles. To spread their spores, they have worked out another collaboration. Ripening truffles emit delicious fragrances of garlic, cheese, or fish to attract tiny forest gourmets. Squirrels, mice and voles unearth these treats,

The next generation of trees is nurtured by this decomposing nurse log.

108 Alder Flat 23

devour them, and inadvertently but effectively deposit their spores throughout the forest.

Lichens are one of the mysteries of biology. They are not a single organism but a unique partnership between fungus and algae. The fungus provides the structure, and the algae provides food through photosynthesis. Lichens love wet conditions, soaking moisture like sponges. When dry, they go dormant and can stay in this suspended state for years, rebounding when moistened.

Photo courtesy USDA Forest Service.

They fix nitrogen from the air, making it available to plants when they fall and decompose. Rodents, deer and elk eat them. Indians collected them as both food and medicine.

Of all the residents of Cascadia's forests, the spotted owl is certainly the most notorious. These skilled hunters have adapted to old-growth Douglas-fir forests over thousands of years, depending upon the layered canopy for cover, and the voles and flying squirrels for food. When all is well with the old-growth forest, the owls prosper. Without its cover, they are easy prey for larger great horned owls. For this reason, they are used as the symbol of these ancient groves and are a measure of the forest's well-being.

If you explore the ponds scattered through this stretch of the forest a tail slap will put you into place. The resident beavers have built and maintained a series of dams, varying their activities from year to year and modifying the local landscape. You can't always count on a beaver pond at Alder Creek, as the beavers gradually eat up the supply of alder and willow and move on to new sites, returning when their favorite foods have grown back.

They are the engineers of the forest world. Ambitious and hard-working, they are never still and seem most joyous when constructing a new home or water barrier. In fact, when researchers enclosed a beaver in a room with mud and sticks and a stereo speaker playing the sound of trickling water, the beaver built a structure all around the speaker. Beavers play a significant role in constructing wetlands which help modify the effects of floods and spring thaws and provide habitat for migratory songbirds, amphibians and a host of other creatures.

24
Black Wolf Meadows, Anvil Lake

Trail #724
The Seasonal Round

Corner photo by Tom Iraci

Recommended Seasons: Summer, Fall
Use: Low
Difficulty: Easy

▓ MAPS

Mount Hood National Forest, Geo-Graphics Mount Hood Wilderness.

▓ DIRECTIONS

Take Highway 224 past Ripplebrook. Turn left on Road 57, drive 7 1/2 miles, turn left on Road 58 and drive 6 1/4 miles. Turn right on Road 58-160 and watch for the unmarked but recognizable trailhead in less than 1/2 mile on the left.

Anvil Lake is not one of the big flashy popular fishing and boating sites in Mt. Hood National Forest. If you want flash, you'll find it close by at Timothy Lake. Instead, this small lake surrounded by wetland, forest and meadow provides a subtle glimpse at the likely setting of an ancient annual ritual that connected, and still connects, the native peoples of this region to the land.

The Indian people who lived along the Columbia, Willamette and Clackamas rivers for at least the past 10,000 years were blessed with a wealth of rich nutritious food. The silvery tide of salmon that fought their way home to ancestral streams each year provided a reliable and abundant source of fats and proteins.

This made the people along these rivers comparatively rich. They were able to catch plenty of salmon to meet their own needs for the year, with enough left over to trade with people from the coast and the inland plateau. In fact, the Columbia River Gorge was a major trade corridor for indigenous people from the entire western half of the continent.

Still, people did not live on fish alone. They needed fruits, vegetables and starches to round out their diets. Over thousands of years, they developed an intimate relationship with the forests, meadows, wetlands and streams that comprise the lands surrounding these mighty rivers. And over time, they learned to "read" the landscape. When a certain plant blooms in the Gorge, it means a certain berry is ripe in the upper canyons or a bulb is at its fullest and ready to dig. Timing is important when gathering a year's food supply, so that each item is harvested at its peak of ripeness, flavor and food value. Skill at reading these signs meant the difference between a family's winter health and comfort, or famine.

Usually the women of each band were in charge of food gathering. Feminine food knowledge was often passed down from grandmother to granddaughter, avoiding the educational tension that so often exists between mother and daughter. Each gathering

Ghostly cedar snags at the meadow's edge.

thimble, salal, service and strawberries and high bush cranberries were also gathered, preserved, and prepared in a number of ways.

Wet meadows provide a variety of interesting foods, including the lovely blue camas that produces an onion-like bulb, tasty either baked or steamed. The roots of bracken ferns provided an important vegetable staple.

The people who today make up the Confederated Tribes of the Warm Springs come from three distinctly different backgrounds. The Wasco people spoke the Chinookan language, fished along the Columbia River, and gathered other foods in the mountains. The Warm Springs people who spoke Sahaptin,

Crimson huckleberries contrast with gray tree limbs.

season opened with a special ceremony to mark passage into that time of year and to thank the creator for providing another season's food.

Huckleberries were probably the local people's most significant source of vitamin C and were used to liven up otherwise starchy or greasy foods. They were abundant and easily preserved by drying. They were even used as bribery. On nasty winter nights, the best story teller in each band might only be enticed to tell his or her tales if someone pulled out a well-preserved batch of huckleberries. Goose, salmon,

lived on the big river's tributaries, fished, hunted some game and gathered berries and roots. The Paiutes lived in southeastern Oregon, spoke a Shoshonean dialect, and depended on big game and gathered foods.

When these bands were moved off their traditional lands onto the reservation, they didn't even speak the same language and had to adapt to new ways of life. But the treaty of 1855 that forced their move, reserved their rights to gather foods on national forest lands. That right is still in place today. The forest has always been used for traditional food gathering by

Black Wolf Meadows is beautiful in any season.

bands from across the region who collectively shared its use. Today, the Confederated Tribes of Warm Springs keep their traditions alive, gathering foods in time-honored ways.

This side of Mt. Hood, including most of the Salmon Huckleberry Wilderness, south to the Clackamas River was a favorite area for the seasonal round of food gathering. The open rock outcrops, lush meadows, and stream corridors grow nutrient-rich young vegetation. Wise land managers, the native people of this region regularly burned the forests to maintain these

clearings. Burning eliminated brush and seedling trees, keeping the forests more open. It also harshly pruned or killed the huckleberries, boosting regrowth of young productive plants and more berries in following seasons.

Moist old-growth forests provided one of the most versatile and useful materials. Indians pulled long strips of bark from large cedar trees. The weather resistance and flexibility of cedar bark made it useful for all manner of things. Women made skirts and wove baskets from it. It was even shredded and used as an absorbent material for diapers and menstruation.

Knowing just this much about the Indian's seasonal round, you'll recognize a veritable grocery store in the mile-and-a-half hike to Anvil Lake. From the rather obscure trailhead, you enter a moist forest of cedars, bunchberry and ferns. The trail skirts Black Wolf Meadow, an exquisite little flowery grassland full of camas in late spring. It serves as deer and elk habitat come fall and winter. On a September visit to this meadow I was startled by trilling resonant tones that echoed across the grassy expanse and sounded like a cross between a harmonica and a steam whistle. It was a bull elk bugling! The sound

Pond lily leaves float on Anvil Lake.

is the essence of wildness and the memory of it still gives me goosebumps. It would have been a welcome sound to native game hunters.

Beyond the meadow, duck back into the woods and wade through waist-high huckleberries as abundant as anyplace I've seen in this forest. In mid September, bushes are decorated with aromatic blue spheres as large and plump as the local bears must be. I saw a lot of berry bear scat, so make some noise in here to avoid surprises. Bring an extra container or carry some berries home in your water bottle for muffins or pancakes—a true Northwest treat.

Hike through fir and cedar forest, cross Anvil Creek, and watch for the sign to the lake, pointing you down the hill. There was no shoreline trail, nor easy access to the lake, but with a bit of scrambling, I was able to stand on fairly dry ground within the wetland and enjoy a shimmery breeze across the golden grasses. High bush cranberry hugged the shores, the only place I've seen it in the wild. The east end of the lake drains into Anvil Creek where archaeologists have found stripped cedars.

Returning to the trail and continuing, you'll come to the other equally obscure trailhead on the gravel 5820 Road, only a few miles from Timothy. My advice is to head back to Black Wolf Meadow, sit quietly on the bleached log next to the trail, munch a few berries or whatever foods you preserve for such trips, and listen for that big bull elk.

Watch for blue camas in spring, blue gentian in summer.

25

Miller Trail, Headwaters Trail

Trail #534, Trail #522

Guarding the Forest

Recommended Seasons: Spring, Summer
Use: Medium
Difficulty: Easy

MAPS

Mount Hood National Forest.

DIRECTIONS

Driving east on U.S. Highway 26 past the junction with Oregon Highway 35, watch for signs to Timothy Lake and turn onto Skyline Road 42. Drive seven miles, to the well-marked junction with Forest Road 57. From the Clackamas River side, take Highway 224 through Estacada, to Ripplebrook. Turn left on Forest Road 57 and follow signs to Timothy Lake. Continue past the lake to the junction with Forest Road 42. The Clackamas Lake Historic Ranger Station is on Forest Road 42, just west of this well-marked junction.

Clackamas Lake Historic Ranger Station is located near the headwaters of the Oak Grove Fork of the Clackamas River. Surrounding the ranger station, there are several historic and scenic destinations and a network of trails by which to reach them. The Pacific Crest Trail, the Headwaters Trail and the Miller Trail intersect and provide easy access to Clackamas Lake, the Oak Grove headwaters, Timothy Lake and Little Crater Lake (Hike #26). You can start at the Historic Ranger Station with

a peek into the life of a forest ranger in the 1930s, then explore other interesting spots within an easy day hike.

People have been hiking through this area for a long time. Just 100 yards north of the ranger station, a 1957 road-construction crew found a tree carved with the date "September 5, 1808." Centuries-old Indian trails provided a well-established route for the fur trappers who came through in the early 1800s.

In 1900, dentist Herbert Miller constructed the first road to the meadow and built a large log summer home and barn. In 1905, the Forest Service was combing the area in search of a site for a ranger station for the newly-created Lakes Ranger District, a 390,000-acre area stretching from Mt. Hood to Mt. Jefferson. The meadow provided grazing for horses, and Doc Miller had graciously provided the road. The first ranger's cabin was built in 1906, welcoming Joe

Headwaters of the Clackamas Oak Grove Fork.

Photo by Tom Iraci.

Graham as the new district ranger.

The thirteen buildings that stand today were constructed by the Civilian Conservation Corps in the 1930s. During summer months, volunteers lead tours through the ranger's rustic offices and cabins that remain much as they were in the early 1930s. Here you can gain a better understanding of the colorful history of our national forests, a history that hinged on events dating back to the arrival of the first emigrants.

The historic ranger station welcomes visitors in summer.

The Oregon Trail brought thousands of homesteaders to the Willamette Valley and life in northwestern Oregon changed radically between 1850 and 1900. Initially, people sought farm land, claiming fertile river bottoms and prairies. Once these lands were taken, subsequent homesteaders claimed low-elevation forested lands and set about clearing them. While the trees provided lumber for homes and barns, they were seen as obstacles to farming rather than a valuable resource.

With few roads and no rails, western Oregon was an isolated frontier. But in the 1880s, completion of the transcontinental railroad and other connecting rail lines changed that. Commercial farming and logging became economically feasible because farmers and loggers could transport their products to market. The Oregon agricultural economy boomed.

Trees took on greater value as the region developed and the railroads provided a means for mills in Oregon to ship lumber to distant markets. Most of the forested lands were privately owned. Despite warnings to Oregon's timber industry to practice stewardship of the forests, private lands were stripped of timber at an alarming rate.

By the 1890s, there was increasing concern that this rapid pace of logging would deplete the country's timber resources, but moneyed timber interests were adamantly opposed to government intervention. In 1891, a group of conservationists managed to attach an obscure amendment to a general land law that passed through Congress nearly unnoticed. This amendment established fifteen forest reserves totaling thirteen million acres. With them, today's Mt. Hood National Forest came under federal ownership as the Cascade Range Forest Reserve.

The Forest Service was established as a branch of government in 1905 and as the country gradually developed its system for managing forested lands, this particular piece of ground went through several name changes. In 1907, it was the Cascade Forest Reserve. The next year, the Bull Run Reserve and the north side of the Cascade Reserve were combined to form Oregon National Forest. In 1924, it was renamed Mount Hood National Forest.

As the Forest Service evolved, it took over managing forests by establishing policies and restrictions in a law-enforcement capacity. Rangers were often called "guards." Their job was to protect the forest from poachers, timber thieves and fire. The term "guard" lingers even today. Ranger stations are often called guard stations and training camp for firefighters is still called guard school.

The period from 1905 to the 1930s was a romantic one in Forest Service history. Rangers lived in remote cabins and patrolled their districts by horseback wearing jaunty uniforms. They fought fires, strung telephone and electrical lines, built roads and rescued travelers in distress. Clackamas Lake His-

toric Ranger Station is a perfect symbol for this period. Visitors can peer into the past and envision the life of a ranger and his family living in primitive conditions in a beautiful mountain setting.

By the 1930s and the Great Depression, the Forest Service had a backlog of projects and was primed to provide meaningful work for unemployed and unskilled young men. Those stationed at the Civilian Conservation Corps camp here created a beautiful and lasting legacy, building the current Clackamas Lake Ranger Station complex, campground facilities, shelters, trails and roads.

After your tour of the ranger station, head west to the Clackamas Lake Campground and watch for signs to the Miller Trail. It doesn't appear on the national forest map but it links with the Headwaters Trail #522, circling the meadow where the East Fork of the Clackamas comes to life. A spur trail takes you to Clackamas Lake, where a rare algae called "mare's eggs" grows. In spring and early summer the meadows are alive with wildflowers, birds and happy, chirpy frogs.

By late summer, the Headwaters Trail is dry and less exciting. This is a good time of year to explore the wet meadow on either side of Road 42, a bit east of the old ranger station. The dragonflies are magnificent and volunteers who staff the ranger station say that ever since the permit holder stopped grazing cattle in the meadow, the kokanee have come back to spawn. Watch for them in September. If you'd like to explore the area further, see Hikes #26 and #27.

Signs match the style of C.C.C. craftsmen.

Little Crater Lake

Trail #500 via PCT #2000 To Timothy Lake Trail #528

Opaline Waters

Recommended Seasons: Summer, Fall
Use: Medium
Difficulty: Little Crater Lake Trail is easy, Timothy Lake Trail is long

MAPS

Mount Hood National Forest, Timothy Lake Area Trails (Forest Service Information Sheet)

DIRECTIONS

Driving east on U.S. Highway 26 past the junction of Oregon Highway 35, watch for signs to Timothy Lake and turn onto Skyline Road 42. In four miles, turn right onto Abbott Road 58 and turn into the Little Crater Lake Campground. From the Clackamas River side, take Highway 224 through Estacada, to Ripplebrook. Turn left on Forest Road 57 and follow signs to Timothy Lake. Drive past the lake and turn left at the well-marked junction with Forest Road 42. Take a left again at Forest Road 58, following signs to Little Crater Lake.

From forty-five feet below the surface of a moist meadow, cold clear water bubbles from a crack in the earth's crust and pools to form a teal-blue opal called Little Crater Lake. This obscure little geologic wonder northeast of Timothy Lake captures and reflects light in a remarkable way, just as it captures those who visit it. Yet surprisingly few of the thousands of people who boat, camp,

and hike at Timothy Lake each summer season visit Little Crater and enjoy its animated flowery meadow.

The Oak Grove Fork of the Clackamas River is meadow country. The headwaters area near Clackamas Lake Historic Ranger Station is surrounded by interesting places to visit—all of them a bit out of the ordinary. Little Crater Lake lies in the northern part of this complex of trails and scenery. From Little Crater to Timothy and back is about 4 1/2 miles. You can make a long loop starting at Little Crater and circling Timothy Lake on Trail #528 and the Pacific Crest Trail (almost 15 miles), or you can hike to the Historic Ranger Station and back to Little Crater Lake, skirting the eastern shore of Timothy along the P.C.T. (12 1/2 miles).

The campground next to Little Crater Lake and Meadow is small and often serves as sleeping quarters for those who can't get campsites at Timothy. But this little campground is a charming destination in its own right. The meadow abounds with critters large and small so bring the binoculars. Elk frequent the meadow seasonally to graze on sedges and can most easily be spotted at dusk or dawn. The meadow also serves as a moist summer home for warblers. Willows and alders along Little Crater Creek shelter yellowthroats, yellow warblers, hermit warblers and red-winged blackbirds. At the forest edge, listen for the raucous calls of Stellar's jays and gray jays. Nighthawks swoop through the humid evening air.

The paved trail from the campground to Little Crater Lake is accessible for small children and elders. An interpretive sign explains the lake's evolution and the viewing platform lets you peer through the crystal-clear water to the preserved logs on the lake bottom.

Groundwater may always have been close to the surface in these moist meadows. Certainly after Timothy Lake was dammed, the water was forced higher. Below the meadow soil is a thick layer of sediment, over a layer of cobble, over bedrock. Some geologists think that Little Crater Lake formed as water filtered through the local hillsides into the cobble layer and formed a spring that bubbles up through the thick layer of silt. The more widely embraced theory is that a small fracture in the bedrock provides a channel through which water is forced up as an artesian spring. Whatever the explanation may be, it is easy to find yourself mesmerized by the intense iridescent blue-green water that stays a constant 34 degrees and never freezes.

Once satisfied with your view of Little Crater, you can continue walking west to a junction with the Pacific Crest Trail, make a left, and head south toward Timothy Lake. You'll cross Little Crater Creek. The high groundwater is apparent here where springs surface along the trail. You'll climb gradually through fir forest before arriving at your first view of Timothy Lake.

The P.C.T. is a north-south thoroughfare from Mexico to Canada that hits the high points of both the terrain and the

Sandhill cranes sometimes visit Little Crater Meadow.

The view from the deck is simply astonishing.

Photo by Tom Iraci.

scenery. Each year thousands of people travel parts of the route and some hearty souls do the whole trek. Attracting adventurers from all over the world, it is a fantastic place to meet interesting people. The P.C.T. continues south along the eastern shore of Timothy, while the Timothy Lake Trail #528 heads west around the lake across the dam and through the campgrounds on the south shore.

When Portland General Electric dammed the Oak Grove Fork of the Clackamas River in 1954, they turned

Tangerine-colored paintbrush near the boardwalk.

Timothy Meadow into Timothy Lake. Prior to damming, the expansive wet meadow must have been magnificent. According to Oregon Geographic Names, before it became part of a national forest, the meadow was a favorite summer grazing site for shepherds who augmented the natural meadow vegetation with timothy grass, giving the meadow its name. In addition to providing recreation for thousands of visitors every summer, Timothy Lake stores water during high runoff that can be released later in the summer to power the hydroelectric dams downstream.

Timothy is one of the best fishing spots in the national forest, stocked each year with brookies, rainbows, cutthroat and kokanee. On summer weekends it is a very busy place, so anticipate a lot of company on either of these routes. If you come here mid week, even during the height of the summer season, it is much quieter. In spring the meadows dance with wildflowers and the wildlife venture closer than they do when there are campers and hikers behind every tree. Little Crater Lake water turns brown in spring, but clears again in the summer. If you come in September and October, the meadows are golden and rustle in the wind, the vine maples are on fire with scarlet foliage and you may even catch the sound of a bull elk bugling. Time it right and from the Crater Creek bridge, you can watch kokanee spawning.

Try to avoid the main hatch of mosquitos, usually in July at this elevation. They thrive in these moist meadows and can be fierce. Remember the nighthawks at Little Crater Lake Meadow? They eat mosquitos and are often joined by bats, both of which can consume 500 mosquitos during an evening's flight.

A thirteen-mile trail circles Timothy Lake with links to the P.C.T. and Little Crater Lake.

27
Pacific Crest Trail

ENTERING WARM SPRINGS INDIAN RESERVATION

Trail #2000
The McQuinn Strip

Recommended Seasons: Spring, Summer, Fall
Use: Medium
Difficulty: Moderate

MAPS

Mount Hood National Forest, Pacific Crest Trail.

DIRECTIONS

Heading east on U.S. Highway 26 past the junction with Oregon Highway 35, watch for signs to Timothy Lake and turn onto Skyline Road 42. Drive seven miles, watching for the cedar arches near the junction with Forest Road 57. From the Clackamas River side, take Highway 224 through Estacada, to Ripplebrook. Turn left on Forest Road 57 and follow signs to Timothy Lake. Continue past the lake to the junction with Forest Road 42 and turn left. Look for the PCT cedar arches.

The Pacific Crest Trail is a remarkable travel corridor along the crest of the western mountain ranges from Mexico to Canada. It passes within clear view of the West's most spectacular sites including Yosemite, Crater Lake, Mt. Hood, and Mt. Rainier. It also crosses lands under different ownerships, managed in very different ways. While much of the trail crosses publicly-owned land in national parks, national forests, B.L.M. and state lands, some of the

Bunchberry and beargrass.

lands along its route are private. Here the P.C.T. goes through Indian country.

If you drove to this spot from U.S. 26, you drove through one corner of the reserved lands belonging to the Confederated Tribes of Warm Springs. You may have noticed signs along Forest Road 42 that said you were leaving the national forest. They didn't announce that you were on Warm Springs land. Most of the information around the reservation boundary is low key. The relationship between the Indian nation and federal land managers is not.

Federally-recognized Indian tribes in the United States are sovereign nations. While they may not be accorded the same status as foreign countries, they are considered distinct, independent political communities with rights to govern their own affairs. When Forest Service officials and Warm Springs tribal leaders discuss land-management concerns, cooperate in fighting fires, or negotiate boundaries, they are engaged in negotiations between sovereign nations.

In 1855, the Indian people of middle Oregon signed a treaty with the United States in which they agreed to give up their ancestral lands, except for the area that was established as the Warm Springs Reservation. The treaty was intended to settle conflicts between the Indian people who had always lived on this land, and the white emigrants who

Beargrass blooms in high forest openings.

were determined to claim it. The Indian leaders signed with misgivings, realizing it was the only protection they had from losing everything to the ever-increasing population of white settlers.

The 1855 treaty secured for Oregon's First People a number of rights, including use of the national forest for food gathering and other traditional activities. For years it was the only legal document that allowed the Indian people to retain a few of their traditional freedoms. It is held very dear to the Warm Springs people and carefully guarded in every negotiation with the U.S. government.

When they signed the treaty, the tribal leaders were given a map of the lands reserved for the Warm Springs Reservation, but were told it hadn't been surveyed and was only approximately accurate. T.B. Handley made the

official survey sixteen years later in 1871, and placed the northern boundary well south of the location the Indians had agreed to in the original treaty. This reduced the size of the reservation by thousands of acres.

Needless to say, the Warm Springs people protested. As a result, the lands were resurveyed in 1887 by John A. McQuinn, who placed the boundary where the Indians had claimed it should be. But that didn't settle the matter. In the intervening years, settlers had homesteaded a good deal of the disputed lands, which came to be known as The McQuinn Strip. The homesteaders requested a special commission to resolve the issue. In 1890, the commission determined the Handley survey was correct. The argument continued.

In 1917, another survey was done, this time by U.S. Surveyor French Mensch who recommended a compromise. He said the boundary should avoid the settled lands and the Indians should be paid $54,880 for the 7,736-acre difference. Thetribal council said "no" and the dispute continued.

In the 1930s the Confederated Tribes took their case to the U.S. Court of Claims. The court acknowledged the McQuinn boundary was correct and that the Indians should be paid the value of the disputed 80,000 acres of land, worth $80,925 in 1855. With interest, the total came to $241,084. But the court said the Tribes had cost the government $252,089 so they actually owed the government money!

A bit of justice prevailed in 1948. Senator Guy Cordon authored a bill that returned to the tribes any money the government made from the land. The bill passed, and the tribes received yearly compensation. Nevertheless, the

Tribal Council was determined to get the land back.

In 1972, the issue was nearly resolved through carefully negotiated legislation, then Forest Service Chief John McGuire announced that the agency opposed it and wanted a two-year study of all Indian boundary claims. Fortunately, at the same time, Oregon senators Mark Hatfield and Bob Packwood were busy shepherding an identical bill through both houses of Congress. It was signed into law September 21. After giving up the rest of northcentral Oregon, it took 101 years for the Confederated Tribes of Warm Springs to secure all the lands guaranteed to them in the treaty of 1855.

How could two competent surveyors come up with such different boundaries? The language in the 1855 treaty said the boundary "...was in the middle of the Deschutes River opposite the eastern terminous of a range of highlands usually known as the Mutton Mountains." It seems that the name Mutton Mountains was applied to one ridge in 1855, but a different ridge in 1871 when Mr. Handley conducted his survey. Unlike Handley, when John McQuinn conducted his survey, he talked to the Indians and referred to the sketch map attached to the treaty.

Today, you can hike through this hard-won strip of the Warm Springs Reservation on the Pacific Crest Trail. The Warm Springs folks have graciously agreed to permit P.C.T. hikers to cross tribal lands as long as they don't stop to camp. It is easy to see why the tribe fought so hard for this part of their reservation, a lovely open forest of firs and hemlocks with huckleberries, bear grass, roses and a mossy forest floor.

The trailhead is easy to spot from

Cedar posts and carved sign mark the P.C.T. crossing.

Forest Road 42 as you approach Joe Graham Horse Camp. Look for the tall cedar arches. The trail enters the Warm Springs Reservation three miles to the south and stays within Indian property for approximately 35 miles, crossing Wolf Pass and the Pinhead Buttes before reentering the national forest again at Olallie Meadow.

CLACKAMAS RIVER SOUTH

Headwaters Collawash, Hot Springs Fork

Riverside Trail

Trail #723
The Clackamas People's River

Recommended Seasons: Spring, Summer, Fall, Winter
Use: Moderate
Difficulty: Easy

MAPS
Mount Hood National Forest, Green Trails Fish Creek Mt. #492.

DIRECTIONS
Take Oregon Highway 224 through Estacada to Ripplebrook. Just past the ranger station (now a work camp), fork right on Forest Road 46, drive past the Rainbow Campground and watch for the trailhead in 1.7 miles. Consider a bike shuttle between the two campgrounds, described below.

Their name was the Clackamas and they lived along the shores of this mighty river from time immemorial. They were here long before there was a place called Portland, or a Forest Service, or a United States. They walked trails that follow the river's course from its headwaters to its mouth. And they, too, must have loved its beauty, its changing moods, its power and its shimmering seasonal migration of salmon.

Hiking the Riverside National Scenic Trail through ancient moss-draped forest on the shore of the Clackamas people's river, you may get a sense of the rhythm of their days spent fishing, gathering roots, berries and cedar strips, and making tools in a sea-sonal pattern that flowed like the river.

In 1806, when Lewis and Clark returned from the coast on their homeward voyage up the Columbia River, William Clark explored a few miles up the Willamette. He met an old Indian man coming down river, a member of the Clackamas nation. The man described his people as numerous, living in eleven villages on either side of the river of the same name, that flows from Mt. Jefferson. Clark was told the river was navigable by canoe almost to the foot of the mountain.

"...the Clarkamos nation as also at the falls of the Multnomah live principally on fish of which those streams abound and also on roots which they precure on its's borders, they Sometimes Come down to the Columbia in Serch of Wappato. they build their houses in the Same form with those of the Columbian Vally of wide Split boads and Covered with bark of the White Cedar which is the entire length of one Side of the roof and jut over at the eve about 18 inches. at the distance of about 18 inches transvers Splinters of dried pine is inserted through the Cedar bark inorder to keep it Smooth and prevent it's edge from Colapsing by the heat of the Sun; in this manner the nativs make a very Secure light and lasting roof of this bark." (William Clark journal entry, Monday April 7th 1806.)

The Clackamas spoke the same language dialect as people from the lower Columbia River to The Dalles. Sadly, they were vulnerable to the diseases brought along that same river corridor by the first Anglo people to enter this region. Epidemics of smallpox and influenza were inadvertently spread through contact with traders along the coast. These diseases killed thousands of native people in the 1770s and again around 1801.

Eventually diseases caught up with the Clackamas people. While they probably numbered 2500 in 1780, by the time Lewis and Clark arrived their numbers had dropped to 1800. In 1855 they signed treaties that turned over to the U.S. government all of their lands from the Columbia to the Clackamas and from the Willamette River to the Cascades. By then, there were 88 tribal members left. The treaty said that those who didn't blend in with whites and other Indians would be moved to the Grand Ronde Reservation, where by 1871, their numbers were down to 55. Today their ancesters are members of the Confederated Tribes of the Grand Ronde.

The upper Clackamas River gets snowy in the winter, and likely its people built their permanent villages along the lower river. They used the area near Alder Flat, Ripplebrook, and the Riverside and Rainbow campgrounds extensively for fishing and seasonal gathering. In fact, the Forest Service limits construction of any new facilities in this area because there are so many prehistoric sites here. The few archaeological excavations done along the Clackamas show several layers of charcoal, tools, and household items indicating that camps were used over many generations.

Rivers make great natural travel cor-

ridors. The first Clackamas River trail used by settlers went from Estacada to Austen Hot Springs—a springs they first learned about from local Indians. Likely the Indians developed the trail to the hot springs and beyond. Today, Forest Road 46 follows much of the original tread of trails used by Indian families heading up river for their seasonal round.

Indian people fished the Clackamas for spring chinook, late-run coho salmon, winter steelhead, and bull trout. From the shore or perched on platforms, they netted, gaffed, and

This rustic bridge crosses one of several small tumbling creeks that join the Clackamas.

speared fish. Today, the fish species they welcomed back for millennia are declining or near extinction.

Cedar was extremely important to people along the river. They carved boats from logs and built their homes from it. In spring when it was full of sap and pliant, they sliced the bark with a hatchet at top and bottom, and pealed it off in a single strip. From this they made roof shingles and baskets, shredded it into strands for weaving capes and skirts, and pounded it for baby diapers. Pealed cedars can be found all around the Ripplebrook area.

This is my favorite old-growth trail. The photo on this page was taken on one of my best trips here on a crisp December day when ferns were lightly frosted, fog swam through the trees, and deer bounded out of sight as I approached. While the day was chilly and I hiked alone, I felt a warm companionship from the spirits of generations of Clackamas people.

To experience the world of the Clackamas people, start your journey at the new trailhead, midway between Rainbow and Riverside campgrounds. The two campgrounds are run by concessionaires who charge a $6.00 day-use fee, so to hike the trail from the middle, stash your bike at one of the other campgrounds, hike to it, ride three miles to the other campground, leave your bike there and hike back to the trailhead. Don't forget to retrieve your bike.

Bagby Hot Springs

Trail #544
A Healing Soak

Corner photo by Tom Iraci

Recommended Seasons: Weekdays in Fall, Winter, Spring
Use: Heavy
Difficulty: Easy

MAPS

Mount Hood National Forest Recreation Map, Green Map #524 Battle Ax.

DIRECTIONS

Travel south from Estacada on Highway 224 for 25 miles. Half a mile past Ripplebrook Guard Station the road crosses a bridge and becomes Forest Road 46. In 3.5 miles, turn right onto Forest Road 63. Following signs for Bagby Hot Springs, turn right onto Forest Road 70 and travel six miles to Bagby Hot Springs trailhead on the left. This road gets treacherous in freezing weather, so call Clackamas River Ranger Station for road conditions.

You're stripped to the buff in icy mountain air. Reaching through the hole in your rustic wooden stall, you rotate a hand-carved dam into the trough just outside, redirecting its ever-flowing hot mineral water into your personal hollowed-out cedar-log tub. As the tub fills, you temper the 126-degree water with cold splashes from a five-gallon bucket you've dipped from the wooden well just outside. When you've blended the perfect temperature, you release

the dam, ease tingling toes into the steaming water, stretch into this rippley old tree trunk, and soak your weary bones in swirling mineral water under the canopy of an old-growth forest. Ahh.

The Bagby experience is one of both sensual high adventure and simple pleasure. Considered one of the finer soaks in the region by hot springs aficionados, it is well worth the drive and hike. In fact, if a hot soak isn't enticing enough, the hike alone is worth your trip. An easy mile-and-a-half stroll from the parking lot, the trail follows the course of the Hot Springs Fork of the Collawash River, providing a wondrous encounter with classic Oregon Douglas-fir old growth.

Beyond the hot springs, Bagby Trail #544 is a long north-south trek that runs the length of the Bull of the Woods Wilderness, from Forest Road 70 in the north to Elk Lake in the south. Starting at 2000 feet elevation, the trail climbs gradually through the forested valley of the Hot Springs Fork, finally reaching an elevation of 4500 feet at the pass above Silver King Lake. It follows some ridges with good views for a few miles before descending to Elk Lake at 4000 feet (see Hike #30). Most people only hike the first couple of miles into the hot springs.

The springs lie at the former junction of well-established old trails. The Molalla Trail which ran east into Pansy Basin, served Indian people of the region as a major travel route. It was the main trail into the hot springs, served as a livestock trail in the 1920s, and has become part of the route of the present-day Bagby Trail.

The Southfork Mountain Trail ran north to south, from Baty Butte to Bagby, and continued south past Silver King Mountain. Both of these trails predate Euro-American emigration and there is evidence that Indians brought their wounded and sick to the healing hot springs.

Prospector and hunter Robert Bagby lends his name to these springs. Standing on a ridge on a brisk morning in 1881, Bagby was perplexed by a plume of steam rising through the fir trees from the creek bottom below. On closer inspection, Bagby found a cedar slab pointing upstream with the word "Hell" scrawled in charcoal. This "hell" and the source of the hot vapor turned out to be three leaky spots in the earth's crust that provide 120- to 138-degree mineral water to those who make the journey to Bagby Hot Springs. Bagby himself frequented the springs, staying here for months at a time.

Hot springs are a bit of a mystery to geologists. No one knows exactly what heats the water in a chain of hot springs that bubbles to life along the entire Oregon Cascade Range. It seems groundwater is heated by partially molten rock along fractures in the earth's crust in the Western Cascades. Whatever the source, they tend to follow fault lines which keeps the hot water fairly localized. It's easy to see this at Bagby, where bathers direct hot water into their tubs, then regulate water temperature with buckets of cold water dipped from a cistern just a few feet away.

The Friends of Bagby Hot Springs

126-degree water bubbles from the earth.

are an eclectic group of committed volunteers who love a good soak and are willing to dedicate their time and labor to have one. In 1982 they struck an interesting partnership with the Mt. Hood National Forest to maintain and staff Bagby Hot Springs. Since then, they have repaired buildings, improved facilities and provided a regular presence at the site which has greatly reduced vandalism and violence. In 1984 they championed listing of the site on the National Historic Register.

The Forest Service Guard station, a cabin made of peeled cedar logs circa 1913, is now listed on the National Register of Historic Places. It is considered one of the best preserved of only a half dozen pre-World War I Forest Service "guard stations" in the Pacific Northwest. Guard stations were often located in remote sites and were important operations and communications links during the summer firefighting season. When Phil Putz came to work here around 1912, he walked 39 miles from his home in Colton, as there were

Photo courtesy USDA Forest Service.

Ranger Phil Putz built the cabin and the plumbing system.

Photo courtesy USDA Forest Service.

Robert Bagby lived at the spring for months at a time.

no roads. Putz worked here for a number of years and built the guard-station cabin. It is a fine example of traditional log joinery used in building the earliest national forest buildings.

The rustic hand-crafted contemporary bathhouses at the main springs, constructed by the Friends of Bagby, replaced the 1939-era bathhouses destroyed by arson fire in 1979. Perhaps the most intriguing aspect of the site is the intricate wooden plumbing system that delivers hot water to each of the four tubs at the open-air lower bath-

house, the five tubs in private rooms at the adjacent new bathhouse, and one round tub at the upper bathhouse. The original version of these little flumes was designed and constructed by Phil Putz.

Bagby is most enjoyable on weekdays and in the cool season, when you won't have to wait in line for a tub. Exuberant visitors who frequent the place on summer weekends often get rowdy. Alcohol and drugs are discouraged, a wise rule enforced by the Friends and the Forest Service. Car "clouting" is a chronic problem at many well-loved national forest attractions and Bagby is no exception. Plan ahead by clearing valuables and unnecessary items from your car. Don't try to hide items in the car. Vandals are crafty and may be observing your actions. Carry valuables with you and keep an eye on them while soaking.

The Forest Service is exploring ways of controlling these problems. Always check with Clackamas River Ranger Station before heading to Bagby.

Photo courtesy USDA Forest Service.

Tubs are hollowed cedar logs.

30
Bull of the Woods

Wilderness Southern Loop
Bagby Trail #544,
Twin Lakes Trail #573
Mother Lode Trail #558,
Elk Lake Creek Trail#559

The Forces of Nature

Recommended Seasons: Summer, Fall
Use: Light
Difficulty: Strenuous, total loop is
14 1/2 miles

MAPS

Mount Hood National Forest, Bull
of the Woods Wilderness, Imus Geo-
graphics Bull of the Woods Wilderness,
Clackamas River Ranger District
Trail Guide.

DIRECTIONS

From the City of Detroit on State
Highway 22, travel five miles on Forest
Road 46, following the Breitenbush
River. Turn left on Forest Road 2209,
and drive approximately eight miles on
increasingly rough and rocky road to
the Beachie Saddle Road above the
west end of Elk Lake. Park at the
campground.

Bull of the Woods Wilderness marks
the southwestern boundary of the Mount
Hood National Forest. Trails on its north
side trace the flow of the Hot Springs
Fork of the Collawash River below giant
Douglas firs, or skirt the marshy banks of
pools within the Pansy Lakes Basin. Its
south side's rugged forested terrain is

punctuated with rock outcrops offering
expansive views of Mt. Jefferson and
several smaller peaks. It is perhaps the
most "wild" of Mt. Hood's wildernesses.

Bagby Trail #544 crosses the entire
wilderness roughly through its middle,
running north and south. Bagby's northern trailhead is the busy route to Bagby
Hotsprings. A mile south of the bath
houses, the trail enters the wilderness.
At its opposite end, Bagby Trail heads
north from Elk Lake, a popular camping
spot managed by the Willamette
National Forest. This southern route
offers a contrast to the classic old-
growth forest found to the north, and
includes unusual plant communities and
open rugged mountain scenic vistas.

Luminescent panellas glow in the dark.

The road to Elk Lake is very rough. Don't try it unless you have sturdy tires and high clearance. Check with the Detroit Ranger Station, Willamette National Forest for road conditions. The lake is popular on summer weekends, relatively quiet mid week, and serene after Labor Day. In fact, September is a lovely time to stay in the simple C.C.C.-era campground. Wake up to misty lake views and hike in golden slanting sunlight. Several trails begin nearby.

For a loop that makes either a long day hike or modest backpack, start on the Bagby Trail #544 which begins along the lake road. Shortly, you'll enter the wilderness and Mt. Hood National Forest.

Wilderness is a designation given by the United States Congress under the 1964 Wilderness Act. That law established a wilderness preservation system with the intent that the country's increasing population would not settle, occupy and modify all lands within the United States. It states that "in contrast with those areas where man and his own works dominate the landscape...wilderness is an area where the earth and the community of life are untrammeled by man, where man is a visitor who does not remain." Under the act, a wilderness occupies at least 5,000 acres, appears to have been affected primarily by the forces of nature, and offers outstanding opportunities for primitive recreation. It may also contain ecological, geological, or other features of scientific, educational, scenic, or historical value.

Wilderness has evolved from setting aside scenic areas like the high Sierras and high Rockies to setting aside ecosystems. Today, areas that were preserved as wild places prior to the madness of 1980s timber cutting, provide views of natural processes that are hard

to see in what the Forest Service calls "managed lands." Bull of the Woods is surrounded by heavily-managed landscapes. But here, if you have a keen eye and are woods wise, the forest will reveal its secrets.

Look for signs of past forest fires. Trees with branches sprouting all the

Birds make the only sounds on a tranquil September morning at Elk Lake.

way down the trunk to the ground indicate that they grew in the open, not shaded or crowded by other trees. The forest understory of chinkapin, ceanothus, and ocean spray indicates infertile soil. Light ground-hugging fires can help fertilize the forest by reducing the understory plants to ash that provides the next generation of plants with potasium, calcium, and micronutrients. But

hot fires that burn trees also burn the duff and sometimes cook the soil several inches deep. Soil microorganisms die and nutrients are lost. These soils may remain infertile for many years.

The vegetation here is varied and unusual. A moist rock basin filters light falling on the gray bark of Alaskan yellow cedars growing next to the muted violet tones of huge noble firs. Their del-

icate coloring contrasts with their macho ruggedness. Giant orange fungi decorate their weathered trunks where old trail blazes have healed to puckered scars.

Up the trail, in sudden contrast, the forest shifts to Pacific silver fir indicating the boundary of that bygone forest fire. Silver fir's thin bark provides poor protection and they usually don't survive fires. The fire either stopped here or burned lightly through the understory.

Continue along the trail, and again the vegetation changes. A grove of alders provides another clue. Perhaps this is an avalanche chute during heavy winter snows. Rock walls and echoes give a feeling of intimacy. Stepping to an outcrop, the scene changes to a rock garden where miniature subalpine firs hug the boulders joined by scarlet huckleberries, heather, and bear grass.

The trail opens to a view into Battle Creek, a valley with no trails or roads, and so essentially no human access. There are few places like this in Mt. Hood National Forest. In fact, it was a spot identified by wildlife biologists as potential habitat for the reclusive wolverine, an animal that uses large tracts of land and meticulously avoids contact with people.

Again a legacy of fire becomes visible on the landscape. A grove of old-growth firs stands out on the north-facing slopes. Riddled with bleached snags and broken-topped trees, it shows its age. On the south-facing slope, the trees are younger, all the same age, and there are no snags. Determine the age of these trees and you can estimate when this slope burned.

At Upper and Lower Twin Lakes, stop and touch the trunks of a truly-ancient forest. While Douglas firs grow rapidly in mild low-elevation conditions, at 4000 feet they are at the upper limit of their range and they grow very slowly. These giants have massive trunks and plated bark a foot thick, ready to protect them from the hottest fire. They were probably growing here when Columbus landed.

Lower Twin Lake is a great stopping point, home to a rich array of mini fauna including dragonflies and newts. After climbing from the lakes, take the Mother Lode Trail #558, a trail that is old and well established, but not well maintained. The steep, rocky knee-busting stretch levels to a more gradual descent. Lush ferns decorate Mother Lode Creek, still running in September.

At the confluence of Mother Lode and Battle Creek you'll find the remains of a shelter and a nice camping spot with fire rings. Take Elk Lake Creek Trail along its namesake where you'll end your hike once again in a forest of giant firs.

▪ DRAGONFLIES

As you take a break from hiking and relax by the lake, watch the dragonflies. But don't even think about trying to sneak up on one. They have all the advantages. First, they'll see you coming, as they have a 350-degree view of the world. Other insects can see only a few feet, but dragonflies have a range of 100 feet. While their vision is keen, their aerial skills are amazing. They have two sets of wings that beat 40 times per second. They can fly up, down, forward, and backward and they can turn on a dime, making a 180-degree spin in two wing beats.

These amazing creatures live near water and are easy to spot in wet meadows or near mountain lakes. So far, 86

Coral mushrooms decorate elderly noble firs.

Catch glimpses of Mt. Jefferson to the southeast.

varieties of dragonflies and damselflies have been identified in Oregon. While adults use their vision and skilled flight to capture prey, their kids are the fierce ones. Dragonfly nymphs may live for five years under water, breathing through gills. They eat insects, tadpoles, and small fish. They can use their tails to shoot water and can extend their lower jaws to a quarter of their body length to capture prey. So if you go wading, watch your toes.

Olallie Lake

Scenic Area

Lakes, Views and Huckleberries

Recommended Seasons: Summer, Fall
Use: Medium on trails, heavy near lakes
Difficulty: Moderate

MAPS

Mount Hood National Forest, Olallie Scenic Area Map.

DIRECTIONS

You can reach Olallie from either Highway 26 on the east side of Mt. Hood, or from Estacada. From Highway 26, take Forest Road 42 south. Olallie is about 32 miles from this junction. Signs to Olallie Lakes will give you two options. The 25-Mile Improved Route will put you on Forest Road 46. From there turn left onto Forest Road 4690. Pavement ends at the junction with 4680. Stay on 4690 and follow it into the scenic area.

From Estacada, take Highway 224 south for 20-some miles. At Ripplebrook Ranger Station, turn south on Forest Road 46. Follow it along the Clackamas River, and watch for signs to Olallie Lakes at 4690, then as above.

The Olallie Lake Scenic Area has likely been a popular destination for family activities for thousands of years. Today, parents and kids come for the scenery and the opportunity to splash, wade, and paddle in beautiful clear mountain lakes. The Pacific Crest Trail

A still morning at Horseshoe Lake.

passes along the crest of the cinder cones and descends to the Olallie Lake Resort before heading north. While this area is well loved in summer, the crowds disappear in September and the huckleberry bushes turn crimson. It is easy to find solitude at one of the small lakes, then enjoy a long loop along the P.C.T., down to the resort and back along the lake shore.

Olallie Lake Scenic Area lies on a high plateau and straddles the Cascade crest at the southernmost end of Mt. Hood National Forest. Stretching between Mt. Hood and Mt. Jefferson, this is a youthful part of the range, dotted with cinder cones on top of a base of lava that is less than two million years old. Glaciers covered this landscape around 20,000 years ago, but remained fairly stationary. Their deposits of broken rock and gravel left this an open rocky landscape puddled with small, cold, pure lakes. Some of the youngest cinder cones popped up after the glaciers left.

Six to ten feet of snow accumulate here in winter. As the snows melt into spring rains, this area receives three times the moisture that Portland gets. The thin soils that barely cover this rocky landscape stay cool and moist through most of the year. The growing season is short, with winter conditions hanging on well into April.

The thin soils are young and low in nutrients, barely supporting the forest

Photo by Tom Iraci.

Mt. Jefferson towers over anglers on Olallie Lake.

of small pines. The open meadows provide clear views of mountains and cinder peaks in all directions and dance with flowers in early summer. And everywhere you look there are huckleberries. Olallie is a huckleberry picker's heaven. In fact, "Olallie" comes from the local Indian trade language term klalelli meaning "berry."

Archaeologists have found remains of Indian camps along the shores of several of Olallie's lakes. No doubt this landscape drew the Clackamas people to the headwaters of their namesake river. It may also have been a destina-

tion of the Molallas who lived on the western flanks of the Cascades. Open meadows, huckleberries, lakes and high-rock vision-quest sites made this an attractive destination for Indian families who spent the late summer and fall gathering foods to carry them through the winter.

In spring and early summer, northern Oregon bands caught salmon as they returned to spawn. Then, as the numbers of fish declined in mid summer, they moved into the mountains, set up camps and collected and preserved foods. Huckleberries were an especially important food source, providing an important balance of nutrients to the rich oily, high-protein salmon diet. Huckleberries provided fiber and vitamins in a form that could be dried and preserved for use all winter.

Mountains were among the most productive places for human foragers to earn a living, providing the best array of highly-nutritious plants. Huckleberries grow and produce best on high ridgelines throughout the forest. Olallie's open rocky landscape is ideal for growth of lush berry bushes heavy with fragrant fruit.

Family groups picked berries together during August and September. Children no doubt enjoyed picking the sweet fruit. Berry gathering served as an important opportunity for life lessons for youngsters whose survival depended upon wise stewardship of precious foods. With stewardship lessons came spiritual lessons, about generosity, humility, gratitude, and reverence for the gifts from the earth.

Warm Springs and Umatilla Indian children were taught a berry-picking nursery rhyme: "One for the Bear, One for the Coyote, One for the Bird, One for Me." Take one berry out of four and you leave plenty for the other creatures.

Looking north, Olallie Meadow frames Mt. Hood.

Sunset on Olallie Lake and Mt. Jefferson.

They enjoy these mouthwatering treats, too. And the seeds spread by mammals and birds help keep the berry crops thriving into the future.

Once the berries were picked, a trench was dug in front of a smoldering log. The berries were spread on tule mats before the log and dried. The result was a raisin-like dried fruit that would last well if stored properly. The huckleberry raisins were easy to transport and could liven up otherwise bland or heavy foods.

After the berries were dry, these same logs were sometimes left smoldering. Berry fields that were overgrown with trees and brush were burned as part of a regular cycle of maintenance of this important food source. Burning was done very strategically, in late fall before the snows. Elders of the tribe would consult with one another to determine whether to burn and if the conditions were right. Ideally, the fire would burn for three days before rain arrived to put it out. Sometimes horses and open rocky landscape here may not have called for extensive use of fire, other parts of Mt. Hood National Forest were burned on a regular basis prior to 1910. Managers of Mt. Hood and Gifford Pinchot national forests are working with their Indian neighbors to better manage huckleberries for tribal use.

We've gained from many thousands of years of berry testing and critique by Indian peoples for taste, storage quality, and versatility. Here are the hands-down favorites: The dwarf or lowbush blueberry, a ground-hugging plant, remains the undisputed favorite of interior Indians who consider it the sweetest and best flavored. Also called *Vaccinium deliciosum*, it grows in wet meadows and rocky ridges and is common above timberline. Red huckleberries and evergreen huckleberries are common in lowland moist forests west of the Cascades. Black huckleberry is flavorful and sweet. Oval-leafed huckleberries ripen early and taste good, but must be carefully processed or they will spoil quickly.

To explore the lakes around Olallie and taste the varieties of berries that grow here, consider making a loop from any of the connector trails up to the P.C.T. then circling down around to the resort. A series of beautiful small lakes dots the P.C.T. route. I made a loop starting at my camp at Horseshoe Lake by hiking up Horseshoe Saddle Trail #712 for one mile to the P.C.T. junction, then heading north on the P.C.T. I made the mistake of taking the Red Lake Trail to the Lodgepole Trail, a boring route that I don't recommend. Instead stay on the P.C.T. returning to the resort. Then hike around the east side of Olallie Lake circling around Monon Lake and returning to Horseshoe Lake along the gravel road.

were used to drag rocks or small logs to make fire lines to contain the burn.

Through this calculated use of fire, the Indians preserved a landscape pattern that maintained their primary food sources. Burned areas provided twenty years of good conditions for huckleberries, large game animals, and other resources.

The Olallie area has never been logged and fires have been controlled since at least 1907. While the poor soils

Look for these books at your local book store. If unavailable you can order direct from the publisher by calling 1-800-541-9498 (9-5 pacific time).

LEARN MORE ABOUT THE GREAT NORTHWEST WITH THESE HELPFUL BOOKS!

COLOR HIKING GUIDE TO MT. RAINIER
Alan Kearney

When you head up to Mount Rainier, this book is as necessary as your backpack. In this gorgeous, full-color hiking guide, Alan provides information on: access, weather, clothing, footwear, flora and fauna, necessary supplies, photography tips, directions to and in-depth information on 30 different hikes. Alan has hiked all 215 miles of trails and shares his experiences, including round-trip mileage, elevation and physical descriptions of each trail, with wildlife, indigenous plants, scenic highlights, and photography tips specific to each hike. Alan Kearney's photography is spectacular and inspiring, it will motivate you to bring along your camera as well. 8 1/2 x 11 inches, 72 pages.
SB: $19.95   ISBN: 1-57188-180-8

RIVER's BEST GUIDE™ TO THE OREGON COAST
Peggy & Mark Day

This convenient guide was written by expert Rivers and is perfect for everyone. The entire coast is covered, broken up into 7 grids, each area is covered in depth. You will find: the best campgrounds—from the most basic to the truly luxurious; diesel locations; dump stations; RV parts and service centers; activities; grocery stores; museums; and a lot more! Everything you need to make your trip fun, safe, and worry-free. With all that this up-to-date guide provides, your vacation and preparation are not complete without it! 6 X 9, 176 pages, color insert throughout.
SB: $12.95   ISBN: 1-57188-070-4

OREGON'S OUTBACK: An Auto Tour Guide to Southeast Oregon
Donna Lynn Ikenberry

Oregon's southeast corner offers a whole new world with its beautiful desert splendor. In this book, Ikenberry shares her love for this intriguing section of Oregon. Through interesting text and exquisite black and white photography, Ikenberry showcases this lovely area. Also provided are detailed directions for auto tours of the area, giving you the freedom to explore this region on your own. Southeast Oregon holds an allure for many people, *Oregon's Outback* shows you what it's all about. 6 x 9 inches, 88 pages.
SB: $14.95   ISBN: 1-57188-043-7

COLUMBIA GORGE HIKES
Don and Roberta Lowe

Oregon's Columbia Gorge is one of the most gorgeous spots on the planet. Its many hiking trails allow you to explore this beautiful area where you'll find spectacular views and sights at every turn—high waterfalls, sheer cliffs, vast fields of spring wildflowers, spectacular mountains, colorful fall foliage. Veteran hikers, Don and Roberta Lowe have been hiking and photographing the Gorge for a combined 85 years, and in this book they share the beauty that abounds in this region. Forty-two hikes are covered, including hike length, elevation gain, high point, time needed, when open, and what you can expect to find along the way. Don Lowe's beautiful color photography greatly enhances this book. So next time you are fortunate enough to visit the Gorge, be sure to bring this book along so you can be sure you explore *all* that the Gorge has to offer. 8 1/2 x 11 inches, 80 pages.
SB: $19.95   ISBN: 1-57188-203-0

DISCOVERING OREGON'S WILDERNESS AREAS
Donna Ikenberry

This all-color hiking guide features 100 of the finest walks found in Oregon's designated wilderness areas. Each wilderness is explained as to its history, outstanding features, accessibility. Hiking trails have been carefully selected for beauty and rated for exertion. Over 200 color photographs! 8 1/2 x 11 inches, 96 pages.
SB: $24.95   ISBN: 1-57188-132-8

COLUMBIA RIVER GORGE
Marty Sherman

Columbia River Gorge—the beautiful, rugged gateway that was such a terrible obstacle for the pioneers. Discover its pictorial history in *Columbia River Gorge*. Shown in striking black and white photos are 110 outstanding scenes photographed from 1867 to 1952. Starting near Troutdale, Oregon, travel up the Gorge to The Dalles while viewing the old scenic highway, steamboats, rock formations, fish canneries, fishwheels, Rooster Rock, Cascade Locks, and much more. Bibliography, 8 1/2 x 11 inches, 94 pages.
SB: $12.95   ISBN: 0-936608-16-1